A Study of
Christian Standards

Written by

KELSEY GRIFFIN
DAN SEGRAVES
RALPH REYNOLDS
RICK WYSER

This book is designed for personal or group study.

WORD AFLAME®
PUBLICATIONS

PENTECOSTAL PUBLISHING HOUSE
8855 DUNN RD.
HAZELWOOD, MO 63042-2299

Printed in U.S.A.

1

Word Aflame
Elective Series

Family Life Selections

The Christian Youth
The Christian Woman
The Christian Man
The Christian Parent

Other Elective Series Volumes

WHY? A Study of Christian Standards
Spiritual Growth and Maturity
Bible Doctrines—Foundation of the Church
Salvation—Key to Eternal Life
The Bible—Its Origin and Use
Strategy for Life for Singles and Young Adults
Spiritual Leadership/Successful Soulwinning
Your New Life
Friendship, Courtship, and Marriage
Purpose at Sunset
Values That Last
Meet the United Pentecostal Church International
Facing the Issues
The Holy Spirit
Life's Choices

EDITORIAL STAFF

R. M. Davis . . . . .Editor
P. D. Buford .Associate Editor

J. L. Hall . . . . .Editor in Chief
United Pentecostal Church International

©1984 by the Pentecostal Publishing House, Hazelwood, Missouri. All
rights reserved.
Reprint History: 1984, 1985, 1987, 1988, 1990, 1991, 1994, 1995
ISBN 1-56722-043-6

CURRICULUM COMMITTEE: James E. Boatman, P. D. Buford, R. M.
Davis, J. L. Hall, G. W. Hassebrock, Garth E. Hatheway, E. E. Jolley, E. J.
McClintock, Chester L. Mitchell, W. C. Parkey, David L. Reynolds, Charles
A. Rutter, Berl Stevenson, R. L. Wyser.

Foreword

NATHANIEL A. URSHAN
General Superintendent
United Pentecostal Church International

"Follow peace with all men, and holiness, without which no man shall see the Lord." It is significant that in these times of sly permissiveness and situation ethics where Truth is used loosely, that this series of lessons should propound strongly matters that pertain to the holiness of God and man. The Scripture from Hebrews 12:14 makes it solidly incumbent that holiness is a part of the characteristic virtue that will qualify an individual for the coming of the Lord. And when we interpret the Scriptures in the light of seeing the Lord, we realize that there will be no revelation of God without the pure attribute of holiness.

In this sequence of lessons the writers are conveying, in the light of the Scriptures, a spectrum of doctrinal holiness and spiritual holiness that will enable you to have a clean insight of the pertinence of the teachings concerning holiness. The desire is not to incriminate, discriminate or deflate any individual, church body, or local church, but rather to follow the admonition of the Lord, "Ye shall therefore sanctify yourselves, and ye shall be holy; for I am holy" (Leviticus 11:44). In II Corinthians 7:1 we are ad-

3

monished to perfect holiness in the fear of God. When we see sanctification by the power of the Holy Spirit belittled and downtrodden, we are concerned that the church of the living God will not depart from the defining distinction which separates the church from the world. Once true holiness is discontinued in a believer's life or when a church refuses to inspire a called-out people, the direction of sainthood becomes confused. Worldliness, worldly attitudes, worldly attire, worldly amusements, worldly fellowship, and worldly integration will pollute and destroy the strength of a church.

I am personally thankful to God that this outstanding selection of lessons will be placed in your hands for study and careful absorption. It is absolutely possible that the instructions that are given within the framework of these references of Scripture and teachings will be the salvation of someone's indecisive soul, and the stability of the doctrine of holiness will be perpetuated in the church.

"We are called unto holiness." (See I Thessalonians 4:7.)

Contents

Chapter   Page

Foreword 3

1. Spirit of Holiness 7

2. Setting of Standards 19

3. Be Not Conformed 31

4. Biblical Teaching Concerning Hair . . . 43

5. The Window of the Soul 55

6. The Christian Appearance 67

7. A Clean Temple 78

8. Worldly Amusements 90

9. Christian Activities 102

10. Sound Speech 114

11. Courtship—Love—Marriage 125

12. The Occult 137

13. Perfecting Holiness 149

Spirit of Holiness

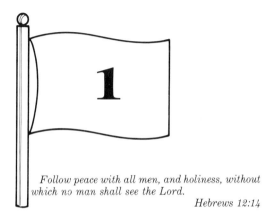

Follow peace with all men, and holiness, without which no man shall see the Lord.

Hebrews 12:14

Start With the Scriptures

I Corinthians 13   Titus 2:3, 11-13
II Corinthians 7:1   I Peter 1:15-16
Ephesians 4:22-24   II Peter 3:11
I Timothy 4:12-13

For many years Pentecostals have sung the words of the chorus written by the late L. R. Ooton:

> *"To be like Jesus, to be like Jesus,*
> *On earth I long to be like Him.*
> *All through life's journey from earth to glory,*
> *I only ask to be like Him."*

This chorus expresses the longing that should exist in the heart of every born-again child of God. The natural desire of every Christian is to be like Jesus.

The key to understanding the message of holiness is found in this sincere prayer of every Christian. Holiness is nothing more or less than being a Christian.

Many church members take on the name "Christian" that have no right to the term. To be a Christian simply means to be "Christ-like." Only as one lives a life of holiness can he be like Christ. It is holiness that qualifies men and women to be Christians. The followers of our Lord were first called Christians at Antioch (Acts 11:26).

Holiness is the most natural way of life for the born-again child of God. "Therefore if any man be in Christ, he is a new creature: old things are passed away; behold, all things are become new" (II Corinthians 5:17). The new man in Christ does not find a life of holiness burdensome or restrictive. The desire for the pleasures of sin is gone and in its stead is the longing to please Jesus and be like Him. It is the joy of the Christian to live a holy life.

With the born-again experience of salvation comes a fervent love for God and His Word. If a person really loves Jesus, he desires to please Him. With the love for Jesus comes a love for His Word and a righteous life. To the same degree that one loves righteousness he abhors sin. A believer will have no problem with sin and worldliness if he truly loves Jesus. Herein is found the secret of understanding the message of holiness and putting it into practice in everyday living.

The Right Attitude and Spirit

We begin to live a holy life by making certain that our spirit is right. If one's spirit is carnal, sour or bitter, it is impossible for him to be victorious. The right spirit comes as one is filled with the Holy Spirit. His own spirit is brought under subjection to the Spirit of Christ. This Spirit baptism is necessary for a victorious, holy life as well as for salvation itself. "Now if any man have not the Spirit of Christ, he is none of his" (Romans 8:9).

The right spirit permits a man to be spiritual and to be free from the law of sin. He will live a life of spiritual victory rather than condemnation (Romans 8:1-2). He will have the correct attitude in his approach to living for God and will entertain a positive position in overcoming the forces of evil in this world.

The believer with the right spirit and correct attitude does not feel the need to question valuable standards of holiness. He will not need to justify himself in questionable circumstances. The delight of his heart is to live as much like Jesus as possible. His questions will likely be, "How can I live more Christ-like?" and "Will this glorify my Lord?"

There are some things that the Christian will not do or become involved with. These do not disturb him, however. His mind will be concentrated on the things that he may do. His whole approach to a life of holiness changes from the negative to the positive.

The right spirit and the proper attitude of the Christian causes him to be directed by godly principles. These principles guide him in living a godly life.

- His love for Jesus causes him to lose all love for the world.
- This love for Jesus creates a desire in a person's heart to be Christ-like in every area of his life—in thought, speech, and deed.
- He focuses his eyes upon Jesus, who is his perfect example.
- He endeavors at all times to be a proper example both to his fellow Christians and to the unsaved.

- He does not judge others with a harsh condemnation, but rather encourages the weak brother to overcome.

A victorious life of holiness is possible if the believer keeps his attitudes right and maintains a right spirit.

Holiness Is From the Lord

"But as he which hath called you is holy, so be ye holy in all manner of conversation; Because it is written, Be ye holy; for I am holy" (I Peter 1:15-16).

One of the great attributes of God is that of holiness. Holiness is His very nature and essence of His being. "God is light, and in him is no darkness at all" (I John 1:5).

In Him there is not even a shadow of darkness. He is perfect in righteousness and moral purity. God can neither sin nor tolerate sin. Only God is truly holy. He is the only source of absolute perfection and true holiness. Since there is only one God, there can be only one source of that which is sacred.

Because of God's righteousness there is a separation between God and sinful man. For this reason fellowship is broken. It is not because God is omnipotent and man is impotent that fellowship is hindered. It is because God is holy and man is sinful that there cannot be fellowship between God and unregenerated man.

In order to become holy we must go to the source of holiness. We can live a holy life only with the presence of God in our lives. Endeavoring to be holy through one's own strength leads to an experience of frustration, defeat and condemnation. It is God who sanctifies and creates a life of holiness. Apart from Him there is only defeat and failure.

When God spoke to Moses, it took the presence of God in the burning bush to make the sands of the wilderness "holy ground." Only the presence of God can change a sinful man into a saint.

Under the law mankind could only become righteous by doing righteously. Under the era of grace one can do righteously because he has been made righteous. In the Old Testament, righteousness was imputed for obedience. In the New Testament, righteousness is both imputed and directly imparted by the power of the Holy Spirit.

It is man's responsibility to bring himself under the sanctifying influence of the Holy Spirit. When a man is cold, he can bring himself to the fire and be warmed. One who is unholy can come to Jesus and be made holy. Through faith and obedience he keeps himself under the sanctifying power of the Holy Spirit. This enables a person to live a life of victory and holiness.

Holiness Is From the Heart

Some believe that holiness is an abstract, mystical, angelic piousness that has no real application in everyday living. Such is not the case. Holiness is nothing more or less than living a righteous, pure life. Holiness affects every aspect of one's life. All of our attitudes, moods, and emotions are controlled by holiness. The manner of a person's conduct, speech, dress and recreation is all a direct result of the condition of his mind and heart.

The heart is the seat of one's emotions, and the Christian's entire life is an expression of what dwells in his heart. "For out of the abundance of the heart the mouth speaketh" (Matthew 12:34).

This is true of a person's speech as well as his entire manner of conduct. What is in one's heart is expressed by the way he dresses, talks, and acts. What is in the heart cannot be kept hidden. If God's presence is there, it will be revealed and will herald forth a testimony of salvation. Others will know whether or not that person is a Christian by the outward expressions of the heart.

If a believer's love is fixed upon Jesus, he will delight in living a holy life. The ardent desire of the heart will be to please the Lord and to be like Him. It will never be burdensome to refrain from sinful practices and to avoid worldly places of amusement. It is a joy to yield to Christ and obey the voice of the Holy Spirit. It should always be remembered that if the heart is right with God, every word and action will conform to the will of God.

Holiness Is a Glory to God

Living a holy life glorifies God rather than self. It always exalts Jesus Christ, the One who dwells within the heart of regenerated man. The beauty of holiness comes from within and radiates forth the presence of God. When one looks upon a beautiful Christian life, he should see Jesus Christ exemplified. The life of holiness is a reflection of the Lord's glory. The Apostle Paul stated that we are transfigured from glory to glory by the Spirit of the Lord. "But we all, with open face beholding as in a glass the glory of the Lord, are changed into the same image from glory to glory, even as by the Spirit of the Lord" (II Corinthians 3:18).

Not only is holiness a glory to God because of His beauty revealed in the Christian's life, but it is recognized that no one can live a victorious life in his own strength. It takes the power of the Holy Spirit to give victory over sin. When a sinner is transformed and delivered from the bondage of all sinful habits, it is evident that it is an act of the grace of God. The life of holiness he lives is the result of a divine miracle in his life. His experience of victory will cause all to praise the Lord.

There is a definite work of sanctification that takes place at salvation. A person is either saved or not saved. If he is born again, he cannot be more born again. As a Christian his standing in Christ is perfect. Yet he may still be imperfect.

A Christian may be blameless and yet at the same time not faultless. He may be living up to all the knowledge and understanding that he has received. While he may be living up to that knowledge, there may be many things that must be laid upon the altar. The newborn babe in Christ cannot be expected to have the same understanding of God's Word as the mature saint of God. It is for this reason that the Lord has placed in the church pastors and teachers: "For the perfecting of the saints, for the work of the ministry, for the edifying of the body of Christ: Till we all come. . .unto a perfect man, unto the measure of the stature of the fulness of Christ" (Ephesians 4:12-13).

It is important for the Christian to maintain an earnest desire to be perfect and to seek God's will in every area of his life.

To illustrate this truth, let us consider a student in school. He might excel in the multiplication tables. If this is as far as he has been taught, however, he would not be prepared to solve problems relating to fractions and decimals.

At the time of repentance, most sinful habits are immediately removed from the new convert's life. The Holy Spirit faithfully convicts and delivers the young convert from the bondage and condemnation of sin. Yet in becoming a disciple of our Lord, there is much teaching necessary for the newborn babe in Christ. Some things may not seem harmful until the harmful effects are revealed by the Word of God or by the Holy Spirit.

Several new converts that lived in a culture where beer was consumed freely continued for a short time after their conversion to drink beer. Then it was revealed to them by the Holy Spirit that this was wrong, and they immediately abstained. Another group of believers continued to use alcoholic wine at their weddings until they were taught that this was not pleasing to the Lord. They discontinued the practice at once.

The Apostle Paul recognized that he was not yet perfect, but he reached for perfection in his life. He stated, "Not as though I had already attained, either were already perfect: but I follow after. . ." (Philippians 3:12).

Paul exhorted the Hebrew Christians to strive for perfection. He said, "Let us go on unto perfection. . ." (Hebrews 6:1).

The saint of God will not tolerate any known sin or worldly habit in his life, and he will walk in all the light he has. He will maintain at all times a sincere desire to be like Jesus and will recognize that a life of holiness involves a continuous growth and spiritual maturing.

Holiness Is Produced by a Heart that Is Spirit Filled

Christian living involves a life of obedience to the Word of God and the voice of the Holy Spirit. The Bible calls for explicit obedience. It should always be a joy to obey God's Word. If one has the right spirit, he will not hesitate to obey completely. Partial obedience is really disobedience.

The twentieth-century Christian has to decide regarding the right and wrong of many things that were unknown in Bible days. The Apostle Paul knew nothing about television, tobacco, and drugs. The Christian should rely upon the voice of the Holy Spirit. As long as he is sensitive to the Spirit's direction, he will never make a mistake. (See John 16:13; Romans 8:1.)

The Holy Spirit will not only give positive direction regarding a life of holiness, but will flash a caution light when one is inclined to do wrong. When sin enters the life of a Christian, the Holy Spirit is grieved and will cause the erring child of God to feel convicted. There will be an unpleasant feeling and a definite condemnation regarding the matter. The consecrated Christian will heed the Spirit's voice and will immediately correct his wrong actions. This will be experienced many times as the believer grows in grace and the knowledge of the Lord Jesus Christ.

There are very few problems, if any, when the Christian obeys the Word of God and heeds the voice of the Holy Spirit.

Holiness Is a Necessity, Not an Option

Holiness is essential to salvation. If the sinner has to forsake sin in order to be saved, the Christian must live free from sin in order to stay saved. Paul wrote to the Hebrews to "follow peace with all men, and holiness, without which no man shall see the Lord" (Hebrews 12:14).

Fellowship with God is broken because of sin. God had to deal with the sin question before salvation could be provided. For the same reason, sin has to be dealt with in an individual's heart and life before he can have fellowship with God. Salvation is maintaining fellowship with Jesus Christ, and when that fellowship is broken there is no salvation. Fellowship must be restored in order to have salvation.

No sin will enter heaven. If sin could enter heaven, it would cease to be heaven. Holiness is living a life of victory, free from sin and condemnation—a requirement for entering heaven.

Christ's bride is a glorious church without spot or wrinkle (Ephesians 5:27). Jesus is not returning for a worldly, sinful church. He is returning for a holy church that has a glorious fellowship with Him.

The Christian who loves Jesus and plans to be ready for the Rapture will gladly lay aside every sin and be robed with the righteousness of Christ.

Holiness Is Compensation Without Compromise

There is great reward in living a victorious life of holiness. We can live above condemnation and have sweet fellowship with Jesus Christ. We enjoy the peace of God in our hearts and live happy lives. We can share this happiness with others, and our relationship with friends and loved ones is enriched.

Because the Christian does not waste his strength in dissipation, he enjoys better health and a longer life. His finances are not spent upon the pleasures of sin, enabling him to practice proper stewardship. He can sleep more soundly for he knows that all is well between himself and God, and he has everything right with his fellow man. The dividends that follow a life of holiness can hardly be counted, for they are so numerous.

The life that is blessed by God is a life that is fully surrendered to the will of God without compromise. Compromise is defeat, and defeat results in guilt and condemnation.

The Christian who will be blessed by the Lord is one who desires holiness because he loves Jesus Christ. He longs to live close to Him and be Christlike in every area of his life. He will never question how close he can live to the world and still be saved. He sees how close he can live to Christ because his heart is overwhelmed with a deep love for His Savior.

A Christian will have no problem in living for Christ and giving up worldly affections if he keeps the proper priorities and sets the right goals. He will discover that a holy life is the normal, natural way for a Christian to live.

Test Your Knowledge

1. How important are a Christian's attitudes in living a life of holiness?

2. Does God expect His children to be holy? List two or three verses of Scripture that identify how God feels about His children being holy.

3. Why is it necessary to always have the right spirit?

4. Is it permissible for a Christian to manifest pride in his heart? Explain your answer.

5. Consider the statement, "A Christian may be blameless but still not faultless." Do you agree with this concept?

6. Where were the disciples of Jesus first called Christians?

7. What is the secret of understanding holiness and practicing it every day?

8. Can a man belong to Christ without the baptism of the Holy Spirit? (Refer to Romans 8:9.)

9. Where does holiness begin in a man? How is it then manifested in a Christian?

10. List some of the natural dividends of a life of holiness.

Apply Your Knowledge

Since the source of holiness is God, the Christian should draw strength from God's indwelling Spirit in order to achieve and maintain holiness. The process is natural and mellifluous when one learns to depend upon and trust in the direction of the Holy Spirit.

Oil check. Here is a project that may help you maintain your Christian attitude. As a car needs oil to function, the Christian needs the oil of the Holy Spirit to maintain a holy attitude. Try the following steps to check your oil daily:

1. *Begin the day with prayer.* This will start you off in the right direction. It is like filling the car's crankcase with oil before a journey. You will prepare yourself for the day ahead when you pray.

2. *Meditate on the Lord throughout the day.* This

will keep you operating properly through the circumstances you will face. As you are aware of God's Spirit in your life, you will more comfortably respond to His direction.

3. *Rely on the Lord when situations arise.* Respond sensitively to His guidance. If you should find yourself reacting to circumstances hastily and relying on the flesh, you will recognize your need to rely more on Him. Relax and allow the oil of God's Spirit to lubricate your heart with His presence. Respond to the Holy Ghost and maintain His unction in your life.

Expand Your Knowledge

Read the Scriptures for the next chapter and meditate on them before continuing in your study. You may wish to research the meaning and origin of the word *standard* before reading chapter two. Notice its close association to the words *banner, flag,* and *ensign.*

Setting of Standards

So shall they fear the name of the LORD from the west, and his glory from the rising of the sun. When the enemy shall come in like a flood, the Spirit of the LORD shall lift up a standard against him.

Isaiah 59:19

Start With the Scriptures

Psalm 20:5	II Corinthians 6:14-7:1
Song of Solomon 6:4	Titus 1:5
Acts 20:28-29	Hebrews 13:7, 17, 24
I Corinthians 11:2	Jude 3

Standards can be of great value when used for the right purpose. Paul taught that the gifts of the Spirit were most useful when administered in love. (See I Corinthians 13.) Similarly, standards will be the most beneficial when we understand their purpose and that they are administrated in love.

The more the purpose and use of standards are understood, the better qualified a person will be to keep them. This is depicted by the psalmist in Psalm 20. He had a close relationship with God and wanted the banners set up in the name of the Lord. Those physical banners (standards) identified him with the Lord. They indicated to others where his strength came from, what he had to rejoice in, and who would fight his battles.

In the spiritual walk there are also standards that identify the church as belonging to Jesus Christ. When people do not fear the enemy, they are willing to wave these banners high. Fear sometimes hinders the vigorous display of the flag in the time of battle. On the other hand, courage and boldness in this warfare against sin cause the church to bravely lift its flag high, telling the world whose side it is on.

Why Have Standards?

The church is ordained to be a light in this world. Light stands out in the darkness and causes the church to be conspicuous to the world. It is noticeable; it is obvious. (See Matthew 5:14-16.)

That which attracts attention to a person is the light others see. Flamboyant clothing may draw attention to a person's flesh and could cause others to misinterpret that person's spirit and true character. In the same manner, modest clothing can control physical attraction toward an individual. This would reveal the Christian personality and allow the genuine character of that person to stand out.

The church is appointed to be the ambassador of Jesus Christ. We should reflect His light and glory to the world. It is the objective of the church to draw attention to the One whom we represent rather than to ourselves. In everything, we should endeavor to be identified with Jesus Christ. Standards, when properly applied to our living, help to bring that identity about. (See II Corinthians 5:20; I Corinthians 6:19-20.)

What Do Standards Represent?

A standard is a flag or banner. Flags represent certain customs and traditions of a country or people. They speak of lifestyles and philosophies of life. A nation desires to project a good image with its representative flag. Its constituents want people to think of their quality form of government, military power and authority, and their disciplines and united convictions. They are particularly interested in demonstrating their uniqueness—those qualities which make them distinct from other nations.

From the connotation of the flag being an identifying object and a representation of distinction came the idea of standards in a moral sense. Standards became a term used for a model or example to be followed. They are the patterns or criteria by which the world identifies our uniqueness and distinction as the people of God. They are flags that let the world know we belong to Jesus Christ.

In battle, the flag identifies the soldiers of each side. Since the church is engaged in a spiritual warfare, it is reasonable that there would be certain flags or standards which would identify the church. The enemy must know that we are not part of his regiment.

Our standards are the symbols which act as a flag to tell the world upon what convictions we stand. These standards have to do with what we wear and how we wear it, where we go and do not go, what we say and do not say. They identify us as disciples of Christ.

Standards represent distinction. God has always maintained a separated people, whereas the devil entices the church to mix with the world. The world, under the devil's influence, is trying the unisex look, but God has always made a conspicuous distinction between the male and female.

Standards help to distinguish the church from the

world. Both in the manner of dress and in codes of conduct the church is different from the world. That distinction and difference is very pleasing to God. To God, our beauty is not in physical features, but rather in the spirit and character of the inner man. How beautiful it is to have God's Spirit radiating from our lives! He said He would "beautify the meek with salvation" (Psalm 149:4).

Standards represent warfare. Standards are set up as a declaration of war. Standards are our military ensigns or flags. Although the enemy is coming against us in a flood of immorality, humanism, perversion, divorce and abortion, the church does not sit idle and passive. The standard must be lifted as our military ensign against the attack of the enemy (Isaiah 59:19).

Although the world of sin may become darker, it will only make the light and truth of the church more obvious. There will always be a people that will stand for righteousness in the face of adversity. They will not be afraid to raise high the standard of the church.

What a banner for righteousness Joshua and Caleb were as they stood before the entire camp of Israelites! What a banner the three Hebrew children were in the fiery furnace! David stood alone before Goliath; Noah stood alone by his ark; Abraham stood alone with his promise; and Joseph stood alone with his dream. All of these were "banners of truth" waving high before the world.

Standards represent quality. A young princess of England was once being directed by her nurse to discipline herself. The child said, "I do not have to do that; I am the princess." The nurse wisely replied, "That is exactly why you must do it."

The church is a spectacle to the world. Life is like a theatre stage upon which we pass but once. Christians are on display, showing the quality of life God has made available. If for no other reason, we should display high standards to reveal the value of God's work in us. He has truly made something beautiful of our lives.

God has adopted us into His royal family (Romans 8:15; I Peter 2:9). Since we are the royalty of God, we should gladly bear the standards of the royal family. Through this we allow the world to see not only our distinction and separation, but also the high quality of life that has been given to us by our Father.

Everything God does in a man's life is for his good; it is for the purpose of transforming men into His character(Romans 8:28-29). Thus, He desires to see the highest quality produced in the Christian life. The standard of quality is apparent through a Christian's life and character. Thus the standards set by the Christian are to be reflective of the high standard of quality he desires in his life.

Standards represent a united effort. Every policeman wears a uniform that looks like all the others that are worn by the men on that same force. All the United States postmen have a familiar dress. Each time you see this kind of uniformed person, he represents one of many. He represents a united effort to distribute mail or control the crime and violence of the city. By the same token, the Christian should have in his lifestyle, his philosophy of life, his character, and even standards of dress, something that speaks of the united effort of the church to live for God. This does not mean that all Christians should wear the same uniform. It does mean, however, that there are certain characteristics about the standards of the church that cause the world to recognize us as belonging to Jesus Christ.

There cannot be a united endeavor without discipline, direction, order, and authority. This is a day in which many do that which is right in their own eyes. Many are dishonest and willfully break the law. A rebellious generation without a moral code is dominating our society. This is a call for the church to arise and show the standard of right direction and order. The church must produce the fruit of a disciplined life and allow the adhesiveness of authority to unify us in our stand for that which is right.

A united effort can be maintained only through submission to authority. The Bible teaches submission to all authority—to parents (Ephesians 6:1-3), to employers (Ephesians 6:5-8), to the government (Romans 13:1-7; Titus 3:1; I Peter 2:13-14), and to the church leaders (Titus 1:5; Acts 20:28-29; Hebrews 13:17; I Peter 5:1-3). The distinctive reference God made to obedience (I Samuel 15:22-23) and His stern action against the rebellious (Numbers 16:31-35) reveal to us His standard of submission to authority. The purpose of submission is to keep the united work of the church operating.

Where Do Standards Come From?

Standards, when set arbitrarily, can cause confusion and division in the body of Christ. Sincere people who desire to conform to the right models and ideals of the church can be hurt and lose their direction. To avoid such confusion, it is important that we understand where and how standards should be set. There are actually several methods God uses to show us His standards.

The Word of God sets standards. The Word of God is the mind of God. It expresses to us the will of God for humanity, as well as revealing the history of God's dealing with men. When we know how God thinks concerning the issues of life, we should have little doubt as to His standards. This knowledge of God's will through His Word is a great treasure to the Christian (Jeremiah 9:23-24; Proverbs 2:1-12).

There are definite principles of God established in His Word which define many of the standards of the church. Many scriptural standards are clearly indicated in the Bible. Others must be interpreted through a proper understanding of God's principles and by rightly dividing the Word of truth (II Timothy 2:15). The more we apply ourselves to diligent study of the Bible, the more we may understand and appreciate the standards that God has set for His people.

The Spirit of God sets standards. There are times when we do not understand what the Bible teaches about certain modern philosophies. The Spirit will often quicken our minds to certain verses of Scripture or reveal certain things as harmful to our spiritual well-being. These times of prompting by the Spirit are referred to as conviction.

Many years ago, when the Pentecostal movement first began in North America, people did not know that tobacco caused cancer. Many, however, felt convicted by the Spirit that it was wrong to use tobacco in any form. The use of tobacco was not dealt with directly by the Bible, but verses of Scripture such as "Let us cleanse ourselves from all filthiness of the flesh and spirit" (II Corinthians 7:1) were quickened to their minds. They considered this habit as filthy to the flesh. Only recently was it proven that tobacco is harmful to the body, but God had convicted His people about it many years ago.

God dealt with His people in a similar fashion concerning television. It looked like a promising tool of communication when it first emerged, and much of the programming at that time could not be proven to be harmful. But God knew how it would rapidly deteriorate into one of the most influential tools the devil has yet used.

Many people felt a conviction against television by

the Spirit when it was first introduced. Now it is obvious, even to the world, that it has been a bad influence upon our society. For years many people were ridiculed by the world for being against television. Now, more and more of those who embraced television are beginning to fight against it as they, too, see its harmful influence.

The Spirit often convicts people. They are sensitive to God and realize a need to conform to the conviction of their hearts. Even if we do not share that person's conviction, we must be careful not to dismiss it lightly or think less of that individual. It is always good to respect the convictions of others.

Where did the standard originate that dictated dress style? It was from the Spirit of God when He came into the Garden of Eden and found Adam and Eve trying to hide their nakedness with fig leaves. Fig leaves were their choice for clothing, but God intervened and made them clothes of skin (Genesis 3:21). God overruled their selection and established His standard for their manner of dress.

Tradition sets standards. Many people who have departed from formal denominations fear tradition. However, there are many traditions that are good to keep. Paul often admonished Christians to "hold the traditions which ye have been taught" (II Thessalonians 2:15). He also taught them to "withdraw yourselves from every brother that walketh disorderly, and not after the tradition which be received of us" (II Thessalonians 3:6). He praised the Corinthians for keeping the traditions (ordinances) as he had delivered them (I Corinthians 11:2).

Daniel would not eat the king's meat because it was a lawful tradition in Israel not to eat meat offered to idols. (See Daniel 1:8.) The Rechabites would drink no wine because it was a tradition in their family. God used this to condemn Israel because this foreign people were stricter in their family tradition than Israel was in keeping the precepts of the living God. (See Jeremiah 35:2-19.)

Sometimes certain standards may be set in the church that are not specifically dealt with in the Scriptures. We must not be quick to discredit traditional standards. Remember that much time, consideration, and prayer have usually gone into the decision to take such a stand.

The standard is generally built upon the foundation of some principle of God and should not be considered lightly. There is safety in the multitude of counsel (Proverbs 11:14). It is wise to revere and respect standards that have made their way into our traditions.

Culture sets standards. Under some cultures the lighting of a candle in church speaks of praying for the dead. In those areas it would be inappropriate to have a candle-light consecration service. Those who had come from this cultural background would be confused and perhaps tempted to again pray for their dead.

Paul dealt with these same problems in regard to eating meat offered to idols. (See I Corinthians 8; Romans 14.) The culture itself dictated certain standards which the church had to set in order to remain free of reproach.

We have faced the same problems in our day with dress and hairstyles. Sometimes the church has found it needful to set standards simply to avoid association with certain elements that were not Christian. There are times that this is necessary in order to maintain the separation from the world that God has ordained for His church.

Certain undesirable groups and lifestyles often become associated with a particular code of dress, hairstyle, or behavior. When this occurs in any culture, the only way to avoid being identified with that group is to avoid the elements that mark them. In avoiding this identification, certain cultural standards become apparent.

The individual sets standards. Every Christian should have certain convictions that fit his own life. Some people have found themselves craving certain things, such as coffee or soft drinks. They thus felt that they should not allow such things to control their lives and thus laid them aside in self-discipline. That is commendable; however, that person should not make such standards universal.

It is unkind and unchristian to ridicule another man's convictions. It is also improper to impose our standards upon everyone else.

When Are Standards Important?

When any standard shows the world what God is doing, it is important. For Noah, that standard was building an ark and preaching righteousness. His faith condemned the world, and he became heir of that righteousness which is by faith (Hebrews 11:7). Standards are important if they point men to Christ. They are harmful if they merely point to a holier-than-thou attitude which God hates (Isaiah 65:5). Christ openly rebuked the Pharisees for their superficial standards (Matthew 23).

Standards are not an end in themselves. When that becomes the case, we become guilty of the world's charge of legalism. We are not to be legalistic. Standards do not save us. They are merely tools to draw attention to the right things, to help us live a life that will save us, and to give direction and order to our lives.

Certain things may be lawful for us, but all things are not expedient (I Corinthians 6:12; 10:23). As we begin to examine our convictions, we must determine what the Spirit has dealt with us about. We must be honest. We must consider what effect it will have upon our fellow Christians, and we must determine whether it is God or ourselves who get the glory. Will the standard make you more spiritual and useful? If it does, by all means live up to it. Will it result in making you a slave? If it does, abandon it for something better. Will it render a valuable service to God, or will it just waste your time?

When a proper attitude is maintained concerning the purpose of standards, we will have a greater appreciation for them. Standards do not serve as a fence, keeping us out of the world. They are the "guardian fences" of God, keeping the world out of us. They help to protect us from the enemies of our soul, allowing us to live a more peaceful and quality life in the Spirit of God. We can then really learn how to enjoy the abundant life brought to us by Jesus Christ.

Test Your Knowledge

1. In its origin, a standard was simply a _____ _____ or an _____.

2. As a flag represents a nation, standards identify the church as belonging to _____ _____.

3. Christians are _____ of Christ (II Corinthians 5:20).

4. Standards help to distinguish the _____ from the _____.

5. The Bible teaches _____ to all authority.

6. List the five things that influence the setting of standards for the church. _____, _____, _____, _____, and _____.

7. The Word of God expresses God's _____ for all humanity.

8. Understanding the _____ of God which are established in His Word helps to define many church standards.

9. Sometimes the Spirit of God _____ people concerning certain practices because He knows the end result of it.

10. The _____ would drink no wine because of family tradition.

Apply Your Knowledge

You may compose a list of standards which you have adopted for your life. Determine the influencing factor behind each standard. Recommit yourself to the keeping of those standards in your life.

The adage "he who stands for nothing will fall for anything" may be appropriate regarding standards. It is good to possess the self-discipline and godly commitment to maintain a personal standard for living. You will be strengthened and blessed by making some fresh commitments to God regarding your life. There should never be a cause to be embarrassed or ashamed of your personal standards and convictions. God will honor you as you honor Him in your life.

Expand Your Knowledge

Chapter three, "Be Not Conformed," will carry you farther into the realm of the biblical principles of commitment to God and separation from worldliness. In preparation for studying the chapter, it would be good to read and meditate on the Scriptures listed under the chapter title.

You may want to write on paper what you think a living sacrifice is as mentioned in Romans 12:1. Write your thoughts on one page of paper and save it for future reference. You may wish to share it with someone else, or you may simply keep it for your personal enrichment.

Be Not Conformed

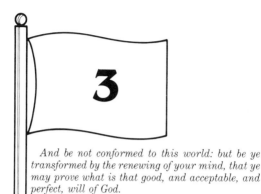

And be not conformed to this world: but be ye transformed by the renewing of your mind, that ye may prove what is that good, and acceptable, and perfect, will of God.

Romans 12:2

Start With the Scriptures

Matthew 6:19-25
I Corinthians 6:9-20
Colossians 3:2
II Timothy 2:4; 4:10

Hebrews 11:14-16, 24-25
James 4:1-4
II Peter 2:20
I John 2:15-17

A great battle between the forces of righteousness and the forces of evil has existed from the time of Adam's fall in the garden.

Every child is born with the Adamic nature and has a tendency to sin. We may remain quite unaware of this fact until we are converted and begin to live for God. Before experiencing the new birth, we all drift downstream and away from God.

We make an about face when we repent. Instead of drifting downstream, we begin to swim upstream, but we find ourselves in the midst of a tremendous struggle.

The Apostle Paul described this battle between the flesh and the spirit in the seventh chapter of his letter to the Romans. He also explained the result of living after the desires of the flesh and being carnally minded. Such a life ends in spiritual death. "For to be carnally minded is death; but to be spiritually minded is life and peace. Because the carnal mind is enmity against God" (Romans 8:6-7).

A person cannot travel two directions at the same time. When he is traveling north, he cannot go south. If he is going up, he cannot go down at the same time. The Christian travels upward while others are drifting downward. Because of this, he may find himself in a real spiritual battle which he cannot fully understand or explain.

There are three principle forces which oppose the Christian: the world, the flesh, and the devil. These powerful forces combine together in attempting to hinder the Christian from living a spiritual and victorious life. The devil dominates the world, and the world caters to the desires of the flesh.

The secret of victory is in dying out to the flesh. The world has no attraction to those who become dead to sin. The Apostle Paul expressed the secret of victory in his epistle to the Galatians. "But God forbid that I should glory, save in the cross of our Lord Jesus Christ, by whom the world is crucified unto me, and I unto the world" (Galatians 6:14).

Love Not the World

The world defined. In the original Hebrew and Greek there are various words which have been translated *world* in the King James Version of the Bible. In the Old Testament the word *world* generally signifies this planet as being habitable and fruitful. In the New Testament the meaning is different.

One reference in the New Testament refers to *world* as the populated world or people. Another word, *aion,* translated *world* is age and combines time with space. *Kosmos* is another word translated *world* which basically means an ordered system.

Satan rules a kingdom which is opposed to the kingdom of God (Luke 11:18). It is this world, a system opposed to God, that Christians must not love. "Love not the world, neither the things that are in the world. If any man love the world, the love of the Father is not in him" (I John 2:15).

In I John 2:16, the world is defined by what it consists of. This also explains why we must not love it. There is a threefold source of evil in the world: the lust of the flesh, the lust of the eyes, and the pride of life.

Lust of the flesh. This is the desire of the body to satisfy carnal lusts in doing things displeasing to God.

Lust of the eyes. The eyes are the gate through which the world is able to appeal to the carnal lusts of the flesh.

Pride of life. This is the most subtle of the three for it exalts self and causes a person to lift himself up in rebellion and disobedience against God.

This threefold source of evil was employed by Satan in the temptation of Eve in the garden and of Christ in the wilderness. In Eve's temptation, the forbidden fruit was good for food (the lust of the flesh), pleasant to the eyes (the lust of the eyes), and desired to make one wise (the pride of life). (See Genesis 3:6.) A similar approach was used in the temptation of Christ (Luke 4:3-10). The devil suggested that the stones should be turned into bread (the lust of the flesh). He then offered the kingdoms of this world (the lust of the eyes). Finally, Satan suggested that the Lord cast Himself down that angels might bear Him up (the pride of life). These devices are also employed against the church. Through these channels, Satan endeavors to attract God's people to the world.

Love of the world forbidden. The Bible states plainly that there is no neutral ground between God and the world. If we align ourselves with this worldly system, we commit spiritual adultery and are untrue to God. "Ye adulterers and adulteresses, know ye not that the friendship of the world is enmity with God? whosoever therefore will be a friend of the world is the enemy of God" (James 4:4).

It is impossible to remain on both sides of the fence in our allegiance to Jesus Christ. When we love Him, we keep ourselves separated from the world. If we love the world, we cannot serve the Lord because the world system is opposed to God. It is apparent that a person must not love the world if he desires to live a life of holiness. The love of the world will hinder one from living a victorious Christian life and it will lead him away from the church. Eventually he will turn back to a life of sin if his love is for the world. Demas was an example of this: "For Demas hath forsaken me, having loved this present world" (II Timothy 4:10).

Demas was a quitter. He was untrue and unfaithful to the Lord. It is difficult to understand how a person can turn his back upon Jesus Christ and forsake eternal life for the temporal things of the world. Demas forsook God because he loved this present world. The sin of backsliding is serious and inevitable when one loves the world more than Christ.

Jesus said, "Remember Lot's wife." She became a memorial of a backslidden heart. She did not look back because she was curious but because she loved Sodom with all of its wicked pleasures. She wanted to turn around and go back. Her heart remained behind with all of Sodom's worldly pleasures.

If a Christian's love is rooted in the world, he will eventually turn back. For this reason the love of the world is strictly forbidden: "No man, having put his hand to the plough, and looking back, is fit for the kingdom of God" (Luke 9:62).

Separation From the World

There is no fellowship between light and darkness. When the light is turned on, darkness disappears. In this same sense the church is light and the world is darkness, and there must be a clear line of demarcation between the church and the world.

"Wherefore come out from among them, and be ye separate, saith the Lord, and touch not the unclean thing; and I will receive you, And will be a Father unto you, and ye shall be my sons and daughters, saith the Lord Almighty" (II Corinthians 6:17-18).

The promise of being received by God and becoming His sons and daughters is conditional upon complete separation. God's plan for His people is to take them out of the world and to remove the world from them. Separation from the world brings victory, power, and the joy of the Lord. The Christian who maintains full separation from the world has a genuine testimony. His life and testimony have an effect upon all who know him.

However, the believer who has a divided allegiance, who tries to live for God and the world at the same time, is defeated and unhappy. He is miserable because he is trying to go two directions at the same time. A divided life cannot continue long. Either a person will dedicate his life to the Lord, or he will turn back to the beggarly elements of the world (Galatians 4:3, 9).

A fine young man came to the Lord and experienced a wonderful deliverance from sin. He had been an alcoholic before God brought him deliverance. All went well for several months until he became careless in his prayer life. He quit his job and decided to relax for the winter months. When he became idle, he thought that he had to find some activity to relieve him from a life of boredom.

His steps downward were swift. His separation from worldly activities started to disappear. He began to attend worldly events again that he had abandoned when he came to the Lord. He became careless in church attendance and began to smoke again. It was not long before he was back on the bottle.

Several years passed and then tragedy struck. One Christmas eve while driving drunkenly home, he was killed in an accident. It never pays to forsake the Lord, for the wages of sin is always death.

This tragic story started when this young man began to associate with the world and to frequent worldly amusements. There are many clean recreations that the Christian may enjoy and not be condemned; however, it is wrong to have fellowship with the worldly and the ungodly. In this instance the atmosphere and environment were harmful to the young man. He became too close to the world, and the world pulled him down into a dark whirlpool of evil. It would have been a different story had he maintained a separation from the world.

In the horse and buggy days, a drunkard had been gloriously saved and the habit of alcohol had been broken. He continued, however, to fight a terrible desire for whiskey. He consulted his godly pastor and told him his problem.

The pastor's advice was simply, "Get a new hitching post."

The man had continued tying his horse to the same hitching post which was in front of the saloon. He took the advice and began tying his horse at the other end of the street. By doing so victory came.

We cannot expect deliverance if we frequent the same places that we partook of before salvation. There must be a complete separation.

In the Old Testament history of Israel, the Amalekites were a type of the flesh. They fought against the Israelites in their pilgrimage journey. The prophet Samuel gave commandment to King Saul to slay utterly the Amalekites and spare none. King Saul fought against Amalek and won a great victory; however, he only partially obeyed. He kept King Agag and some of the best of the sheep and cattle alive. This displeased the Lord and Saul lost his throne.

Where the world and the flesh are concerned, God is still telling His people to "slay utterly." It is dangerous to leave one sinful habit alive. Only a complete separation from the world can assure us of victory.

Conform Not to the World

"And be not conformed to this world: but be ye transformed by the renewing of your mind, that ye may prove what is that good, and acceptable, and perfect, will of God" (Romans 12:2).

Pull of the world. Living close to the world is very dangerous. When a Christian lives in close proximity to the world, the attractions may easily overcome him. He may find himself dragged down into the quicksands of evil desires. The lust of the flesh and the lust of the eyes can become too strong for a weak believer, and he can be swept back into a life of sin. Just as one cannot play with fire without getting burned, so a person cannot flirt with the things that cater to the lust of the flesh without being overtaken in sin.

The physical law of gravity states that two objects attract each other inversely, proportional to the square of the distance between their centers. In other words the closer two objects are, the greater the attraction. This is also true spiritually. The closer a person lives to the world the more he is attracted by the world and the stronger he finds the pull of the world. It is essential to get into a spiritual orbit and beyond the pull of the world.

A gentleman once advertised for a coachman to drive his wife and family. Several applicants appeared and each of them was tested in the same manner.

Nearby, the road ran along the top of a steep cliff. Each coachman was told to see how close he could drive the horses to the edge of the cliff. One after another took the reins and guided the horses and coach at the very edge of the cliff. Finally, one young man climbed into the driver's seat and drove the horses on the opposite side of the road as far from the cliff as possible.

"You are hired," this young man was told. The gentleman was going to trust into his hands the lives of his wife and children. He was not interested in how close he could drive to danger but how far he could stay away from it.

This is also a good policy for the Christian. There is safety in putting distance between us and temptation. The Bible states for us to "Flee fornication." Run from it. Joseph did this when he ran from Potiphar's wife. The greater the distance, the less attraction there is to the world.

Peer pressure. The Christian also battles with the third force in the world, the pride of life.

No one desires to be different from the crowd. Who wants to be considered an oddity? The fear of ridicule, sneers, and teasing has caused some Christians to lose out with God. It is not easy to lose friends and stand alone for one's convictions. However, if he loves Jesus Christ, the Christian will be willing to stand up and be counted. He will not be one of the crowd or run with the gang. He will have a firm purpose and dare to make it known.

Not conformed but transformed. Conformity means to be similar in form and character. If a person conforms to this world, he yields, consents, and adjusts to worldly standards.

Worldly conformity does not necessarily mean that some gross wicked thing is committed. It is a way of thinking as well as doing. When one does not conform, he can be transformed by the renewing of his mind. When his thought patterns have been made new, his entire style of living will change. This transformation shows up in one's speech and manner of dress. The Christian dresses modestly and looks like a Christian should. He does not laugh at smutty stories. The Christian will desire to be punctual and faithful on the job, and honest in all his business transactions. He refuses to tell a lie even if it means he will lose his job. The Christian has no desire for worldly parties or fellowship with the ungodly, and he chooses carefully what he reads and listens to on the radio. In fact, his entire life will be transformed because his very thoughts are being controlled by the Holy Spirit. (See Romans 8:5-6.)

The dedicated Christian takes a strong stand of nonconformity to the world. He proves that this is the way of victory and power. Compromise only weakens his stand for Christ and causes him to give in again to the pressure of the world. Worldly conformity dulls his conscience and spiritual sensitivity. It is best to have strong convictions and maintain a high standard of holiness.

Love for the Sinner

Jesus gave the perfect example of having the right attitude toward the unsaved. We love the sinner, but we do not love his sin. Our separation from the world does not mean that we no longer have a love for souls. The love of God is our example to follow: "For God so loved the world, that he gave his only begotten Son, that whosoever believeth in him should not perish, but have everlasting life" (John 3:16).

God's love for the lost of this world should stir and move us to dedicate ourselves to reach the unsaved. As we see the unsaved around us, we should be moved with compassion. Like the Good Samaritan, we go where the sinner is to minister to him the gospel of salvation. In order to reach the unsaved, we must communicate with those in the world, but this never means compromising with the world. We can only keep an effective ministry as long as we maintain a strong testimony of separation from the world.

The Christian's Place in the World

We cannot isolate ourselves and withdraw ourselves from the world. We must occupy until Jesus comes. It is possible to be in the world but not of the world. The presence of the church in any community has a sanctifying influence.

Jesus told His disciples they were the salt of the earth. The Christian exerts an influence for good upon all who know him. When the sinner is in trouble and needs a friend in whom he may confide and with whom he may consult, he will turn to a Christian in whom he has confidence. The Christian life should be so consistent that the confidence will never be broken.

A young Christian attended a wedding in the community where he lived. Everyone was friendly, but he sensed a certain uneasiness, so he made his excuses and departed. As soon as he was out the door, he heard them tuning the fiddles for the dance. He was thankful that his unsaved neighbors had sufficient respect that they delayed starting the dance until he left. This is the kind of influence that Christians should have in the world.

A worldly church would be a powerless church that could never minister to a lost world. Before a Christian can lift his fellow man, he must live on a higher level. If he conforms to the world he will be dragged down into the world.

The whole issue of whether a man conforms to the world is settled by his heart. If he loves the world he will certainly conform to the fashions of the world. If he loves Jesus Christ he will separate himself from the world and live a life pleasing to the Lord. The battle is lost or won in a man's heart. If he sets his heart upon pleasing Jesus, it will be easy to have a high standard of holiness.

Test Your Knowledge
True or False

_____1. The only way to have victory and power in the Christian walk is through complete spiritual separation from the world.

_____2. The battle between righteousness and the forces of evil is a relatively new development.

_____3. To be carnally minded is death, but to be spiritually minded is life and peace.

_____4. The world, the flesh, and the devil are three forces which oppose the Christian.

_____5. One meaning of the word *world* is an ordered system, which refers to the system of this world which is opposed to God.

_____6. There is a threefold source of evil in the world: the lust of the flesh, lust of the eyes, and the pride of life.

_____7. Because of her complete separation from worldly affairs, Lot's wife was an outstanding example of a Christian.

_____8. The promise of being received by God and becoming His children is unconditional.

_____9. Separation from the world brings victory, power, and the joy of the Lord to a Christian.

_____10. Living close to the world is dangerous for the Christian because he experiences a powerful attraction and allurement toward sin.

Apply Your Knowledge

Although Christians are commanded not to love the world (its evil systems), they are supposed to love the people of the world. The purpose of the church on earth is to be a mighty evangelical army, bringing the lost to Jesus Christ.

Try showing your love to someone this week. Send someone a special card to let them know you are thinking of them and care. Another possibility would be to invite someone to dinner who does not know Jesus Christ in the power of His Spirit. Winning their friendship and trust is the first step to winning their soul to Jesus. You do not have to conform to worldly principles to show them the love of Jesus Christ.

Expand Your Knowledge

If possible, locate a copy of the book *Women's Hair—The Long and Short of It,* by Daniel L. Segraves. This excellent book will help you in your study of the next chapter on hair. It may be ordered from Word Aflame Press, 8855 Dunn Road, Hazelwood, Missouri 63042.

Further research on the subject of veils and hair in Bible times would be very beneficial. It is helpful to know something about the customs of other times. Be sure to read *Start With the Scriptures* for chapter four before beginning your study.

Biblical Teaching Concerning Hair

But I would have you know, that the head of every man is Christ; and the head of the woman is the man; and the head of Christ is God.

I Corinthians 11:3

Start With the Scriptures

Matthew 26:39
Acts 15:1-29
I Corinthians 8:13; 11:1-16

Ephesians 5:21-33
I Thessalonians 5:22
I Timothy 2:8-15

The Bible uses many earthly, tangible objects to represent spiritual truth.

For example, the bread and fruit of the vine used in Communion represent the body and blood of our Lord. (See I Corinthians 11:23-26.) The manna eaten by the Israelites represented spiritual food, the miraculously supplied water symbolized spiritual drink, and the rock from which the water flowed was a type of Christ. (See I Corinthians 10:3-4.)

To a large degree, the system of laws given to

Moses was a system of symbols. Many of the things about the Tabernacle prefigured spiritual realities which were to come in the future: "Which was a figure for the time then present. . ." (Hebrews 9:9); "For Christ is not entered into the holy places made with hands, which are the figures of the true. . ." (Hebrews 9:24).

It must be remembered that the symbol is not the reality, but at the same time the symbol must never be disregarded or treated lightly. By its association with that which is holy, the symbol itself takes on a great sacredness.

For instance, the rock from which the Israelites drank was a literal rock. On two occasions water came from it. The first time, Moses was commanded to smite the rock. He did, and water came out. (See Exodus 17:1-7.) On the second occasion, God instructed Moses to speak to the rock; however, Moses struck the rock twice. Though water came forth, God said to Moses, "Because ye believed me not. . .ye shall not bring this congregation into the land. . ." (Numbers 20:12).

Why was it so important that Moses treat the rock according to instructions? The rock represented Christ, and He was to be smitten but once for our sins. After that smiting at Calvary, the believer can speak to the Lord in prayer and receive His provisions. Moses disobeyed and was not permitted to enter the Promised Land.

Submission to Authority

This chapter deals with a spiritual reality which is represented by the length of one's hair. Sincere Christians cannot afford to discount or ignore the significance of the symbol of hair. To do so is to disregard that for which the symbol stands.

The subject of I Corinthians 11:1-16 is authority— not veils or even hair. Paul said, "But I would have you know, that the head of every man is Christ; and the head of the woman is the man; and the head of Christ is God" (verse 3).

There are three authority-submission relationships:

- Man is under the authority of Christ.
- Woman is under the authority of man.
- Christ is under the authority of God.

The phrase, "the head of Christ is God," refers to the relationship between the humanity and deity. Jesus Christ was God (deity) manifest in the flesh (humanity) (I Timothy 3:16). The humanity was submitted to the deity. This explains Jesus' prayer, "O my Father, if it be possible, let this cup pass from me: nevertheless not as I will, but as thou wilt" (Matthew 26:39).

That which represents the submission of Christ to God is the *flesh*.

Hair Is the Symbol of Submission

What represents the submission of man to Christ? The answer is seen in I Corinthians chapter eleven. "Every man praying or prophesying, having his head covered, dishonoureth his head. . .For a man indeed ought not to cover his head, forasmuch as he is the image and glory of God. . .Doth not even nature itself teach you, that, if a man have long hair, it is a shame unto him?" (I Corinthians 11:4, 7, 14).

There is clearly something about the covering of a man's head—even about the length of his hair— that represents his submission to Christ!

What has God chosen to represent the submission of woman to man? The answer is also found in I Corinthians 11: "But every woman that prayeth or prophesieth with her head uncovered dishonoureth her head: for that is even all one as if she were shaven. For if the woman be not covered, let her also be shorn: but if it be a shame for a woman to be shorn or shaven, let her be covered. . .but the woman is the glory of the man. . .For this cause ought the woman to have power on her head because of the angels. . .Judge in yourselves: is it comely that a woman pray unto God uncovered? . . .But if a woman have long hair, it is a glory to her: for her hair is given her for a covering" (I Corinthians 11:5-7, 10, 13, 15).

It is plain that there is something about the covering of a woman's head—even about the length of her hair—that represents submission to man!

The relationship of authority and submission is the spiritual reality. The symbol has to do with the covering of the head.

It would be a mistake for either a man or a woman to adhere to a symbol while not fulfilling that which is symbolized. But it would be equally erroneous for a person to assume that he could fulfill the reality of submission with the symbol which God has chosen to represent it.

These facts emerge from a study of I Corinthians 11:1-16:

- It is a shame for a man to pray or prophesy with his head covered. It is a shame for a man to have long hair.
- It is a shame for a woman to be shorn, shaven, or uncovered. Her long hair is a glory to her and is given to her for a covering.

Definition of Long Hair

The Greek word that is translated "long hair" is the same in both verses—*koma*. Whatever long hair is for a woman, it also is for a man. This word is a verb, and in both verses fourteen and fifteen, it is translated "have long hair." The word is defined "wear long hair; let one's hair grow long" (*Shorter Lexicon of the Greek New Testament,* Gingrich, The

University of Chicago Press); "to let the hair grow; have long hair" (*Thayer's Greek-English Lexicon of the New Testament,* Thayer, Baker Book House); "to let the hair grow long; to wear long hair" (*Expository Dictionary of New Testament Words,* Vine, Revell).

It is obvious from these definitions that long hair is hair which has been allowed to grow. A person cannot cut his hair and allow it to grow at the same time.

The fact that long hair is uncut hair is also seen in verse six: "But if it be a shame for a woman to be shorn or shaven, let her be covered." There can be no debate about the meaning of the word *shaven,* but what does *shorn* mean? The word *shorn* is, of course, the past participle of the word *shear.* It is translated from the Greek word *keiro,* meaning "to have one's hair cut" (*Shorter Lexicon of the Greek New Testament,* Gingrich, The University of Chicago Press).

There is yet another word in the passage which should be considered. It is a noun, the Greek word *kome,* translated "hair" in the latter part of verse 15: "for her hair is given her for a covering." In commenting on this passage, Paul Ferguson, M.Div., says, "According to the passages cited by Bauer and Moulton and Milligan's *Vocabulary of Greek New Testament* 'kome' is uncut hair. The passages cited by these works where this word occurs in Greek literature demand a meaning of 'uncut hair.'" He goes on to say that the word is used to describe the Nazarites, who were forbidden to cut their hair.

Evidence points to the fact that the "long hair" spoken of in these verses of Scripture is uncut hair—hair which has been allowed to grow. Indeed, the *New International Version* and *Today's English Version* both translate the Greek word *keiro* as "cut."

Plainly, the words *shorn* and *long* are used as opposites. Since *keiro* means to "have one's hair cut" and *kome* means "uncut hair," there is no doubt that a Christian woman should not cut her hair. If she cuts her hair, regardless of the amount, her hair has been shorn. This is a shame and it breaks the symbolism of authority and submission. Long hair does not refer to hair of a specific length (if it did, the Scriptures would have to spell out exactly what that length was so that women could conform), but to hair which has been allowed to grow, uncut.

Significance of the Veil

How is the subject of wearing veils related to this passage of Scripture? And what significance does this have for us today?

The Pulpit Commentary indicates that for a woman to appear in a public assembly with her head uncovered "was against the national custom of all ancient communities. . . . If a woman appeared in public unveiled, she was deemed immodest. . .by discarding the head-covering a woman put herself in the class of the disreputable."

It seems unanimously agreed that the Grecian custom at Corinth was that respectable women wore their veils as a sign of modesty and decorum. The population of Corinth, however, was quite mixed and the customs varied.

It has been variously suggested that public prostitutes advertised their availability by appearing in public unveiled. Women convicted of immorality were shaved and sentenced to this public, bareheaded display of their guilt. Heathen priestesses "prophesied" unveiled, with disheveled hair.

The ethnically mixed population of the Corinthian church was probably a basis for some confusion on the wearing of veils since their customs varied so greatly. M. R. Vincent in his *Word Studies in the*

New Testament (Volume III, p. 246), goes into much discussion of hair and the veil, but the only clear conclusion is that the customs regarding the veil at that time in the Christian world varied greatly among both men and women. Paul was not trying to change these customs, but he was showing God's international means of making the distinction between the man and woman and to reveal relationships of authority.

Should Christian women today wear veils? Although women who wear veils today should not be condemned for the practice, neither the Scriptures nor present customs mandate the wearing of veils. There are several reasons why it is not necessary for Christian women of our society to wear a veil.

No veil was required in the beginning. One basic principle in biblical interpretation is that of *first mention.* This principle says that the first time a thing is mentioned in Scripture it will contain the basic truth which will be reflected in all subsequent passages.

When God created Adam and Eve, He did not instruct Eve to wear an artificial veil. Even after their sin and expulsion from the garden, we read nothing of Eve being commanded to veil herself, even though God intervened in the fashion in which they would dress themselves. (See Genesis 3:21.)

Veiling was but a temporary custom. It has not been followed from ancient history, nor has it been widely practiced during the past many centuries. If a certain thing is a mark of immorality in a specific culture, a Christian woman should not do it. But that does not mean that other Christian women, at other places and times, must refrain from the practice if it has no improper connotations in their respective societies. Culture bears much significance in the traditions and standards of a particular region.

The Interpreter's Dictionary of the Bible, Volume IV, page 747, states, "There is relatively little material on veils worn by women in the Old Testament. The Talmud has no designation for 'veil.' The veiled ladies in the present-day Muslim communities would have been out of place, for the most part, in Old Testament times."

A woman's long hair is given to her for a covering (I Corinthians 11:15). The Greek preposition *anti* is translated "for" in this verse in the phrase "her hair is given her for a covering." The literal meaning of *anti* is "instead of." This is confirmed by Gingrich in the work quoted earlier, by *Dana and Mantey's Grammar, Bauer's Lexicon, Thayer's Lexicon,* and other reputable works.

Since God has provided women with a natural covering of long hair, it is not necessary that Christian women follow the custom of wearing a veil. They are already veiled with their natural covering that God has given all women to show their subjection to authority. If the Christian women of Corinth did indeed wear veils, it was an incidental matter of custom and not the subject of Paul's writing in the eleventh chapter of I Corinthians. He clearly indicates that a woman should be covered when she prays and that covering is her long hair. This symbolizes her subjection to the man, which is her spiritual head or authority.

Those who believe a woman should wear a second covering appeal to the Greek text: "The word translated "covering" in verse fifteen is not *katakalupto,* as in the earlier verses, but *peribolaion.* If in God's reckoning the hair is the veiling, we could rightfully expect this statement to read thus: 'Her hair is given her for a *katakalupto*' (veil)" (*The Significance of the Christian Woman's Veiling,* Merle Ruth, Calvary Publications Inc., Millersburg, OH).

This overlooks the fact that the Greek *katakalupto* (be covered, verse 6) is a verb; *peribolaion* (covering, verse 15) is a noun. The two words are not interchangeable. Indeed, no Greek word for "covering" appears in verses five and six. The words *uncovered* and *covering* (noun) is not specified until verse fifteen where Paul identifies the covering as being the woman's long hair.

What did Paul mean when he said, "But if any man seem to be contentious, we have no such custom, neither the churches of God" (I Corinthians 11:16)?

He certainly was not negating his previous instruction by saying, "I have told you what I believe, but if you don't agree with it, do as you please." Rather, Paul knew some would be contentious and want to reject this teaching, so he anticipated their response by saying, in effect, "We have no such custom as to allow women to pray or prophesy uncovered; their long hair is given to them for a covering."

Men's Hair

What about men's hair? Scripture is equally as concerned with this subject as it is with women's hair. "Doth not even nature itself teach you, that, if a man have long hair, it is a shame unto him?" (I Corinthians 11:14). As mentioned earlier, the same Greek word, *koma,* is used for long hair in verse fourteen and in verse fifteen. Thus, whatever long hair is for women, it is also for men.

It has been seen that the long hair which is a glory to a woman is uncut hair. Likewise the long hair which is a shame to a man is uncut hair.

Does this mean that men may wear their hair as long as they wish, as long as they cut it? Although it is true that no exact length has been established by the Scriptures, Paul taught that nature or instinct teaches us it is a shame for a man to let his hair grow long. There is something instinctive that has caused most men through the ages to keep their hair trimmed short. Seldom has long hair been considered fashionable on men and generally it has been associated with rebellion and indifference.

Customs affect the standards of the church by necessity, but the church must be careful not to be identified with worldliness. Men today should keep their hair neatly trimmed because of the significance of longer hair in our society.

A Christian male will not want to be identified with that which has been a clear symbol of rebellion and rejection of authority. In this generation, longer hair for men was born out of the rebellion of the sixties, spawned by the rock groups, and further developed during the campus riots. It was not brought into our society by moral or godly men.

Paul's admonition to the Thessalonicans appropriately addresses the need here: "Abstain from all appearance of evil" (I Thessalonians 5:22). He also emphasized the proper attitude of a Christian toward that which is questionable when he said, "Wherefore, if meat make my brother to offend, I will eat no flesh while the world standeth, lest I make my brother to offend" (I Corinthians 8:13).

The Lord gave the church authority to rule on matters which may not be specifically addressed in Scripture. (See Matthew 18:18.) This authority was used in Acts 15. It is the consensus of Spirit-filled, truth-embracing pastors that men should keep their hair neatly and closely cut.

What about facial hair for men? As with the question of longer hair for men, we do not pretend that the Scriptures give specific instructions. But all that we have just studied applies to this issue.

It was not fashionable in our generation in Western society to wear beards or mustaches until the social upheaval of the sixties, which continued into the seventies. The same elements which introduced longer hair for men brought facial hair to the forefront as a visible symbol of rebellion and loose living.

The basic issue at hand is that of submission to authority. There are God-given symbols of this submission which we dare not violate, and there are symbols which are widely accepted among men which we would be foolish to violate.

Though a person fulfills every external symbol, his eternal destiny is in danger if he is a rebel at heart. If he is truly submitted to God-ordained authority, he will wish to fulfill every external symbol, whether ordained of God or recognized by men.

Test Your Knowledge

1. The primary passage of Scripture concerning the length of men's and women's hair is found in I Corinthians chapter _____.

2. Although hair is used in the chapter as an illustration, the main subject of discussion is ____ _____.

3. According to the Apostle Paul, a Christian's submission to authority is symbolized by the length of his _____.

4. The head, or authority of every man is _____.

5. The head, or authority of the woman is the _____.

6. When a man prays or prophesies with his head covered, he dishonors _____.

7. The Greek word *koma,* which is translated "long hair," simply means _____.

8. A woman's _____ _____ is given to her for a covering.

9. Christian men should not wear long hair because they do not want to be identified with _____ or _____ _____.

10. A good scriptural motto concerning questions regarding hair would be to "abstain from all _____ of evil."

Apply Your Knowledge

Realizing now the importance of I Corinthians chapter eleven, and that its basic theme is submission to authority, you may try an experiment of submission.

If you are married, try doing several totally unexpected things for your companion. You may be pleasingly surprised how much it spices up your marital relationship. This is usually a sure-fast way to touch your companion's heart and enhance your marriage.

If you are single, try doing some unexpected things for your parents. Even if you no longer live at home, it will be appreciated very much and will probably greatly enhance your relationship with them.

Nothing warms the heart quite like surprising another person with an unexpected act of kindness. You may be surprised how you are blessed when you bless others.

Expand Your Knowledge

Before continuing, consider a trip to the local library for a research project.

Look through the last few issues of several news magazines such as *Time* or *Newsweek* for articles pertaining to modern television. Categorize and analyze your results. You may be surprised to observe an awakening among many people of the dangers involved in constant television viewing.

Many recent books address this issue as well. You may also wish to read a recent publication dealing with this vital problem.

The Window of the Soul

The light of the body is the eye: if therefore thine eye be single, thy whole body shall be full of light. But if thine eye be evil, thy whole body shall be full of darkness. If therefore the light that is in thee be darkness, how great is that darkness!

Matthew 6:22-23

Start With the Scriptures

Deuteronomy 7:26
Job 31:1
Psalm 101:3
Proverbs 27:20
Matthew 18:9

Luke 11:34
I Corinthians 3:16-17;
  6:9-11, 15-20
II Peter 2:14-15
I John 2:15-17

Since ninety-six out of one hundred Americans own a television set (more than own refrigerators or kitchen ranges), the church must educate and inform its membership of the many dangers and evils of this modern medium of communication.

Only a few religious bodies such as the United Pentecostal Church have gone on record as disapproving television in the homes of church members. Those who have opposed television would probably agree that the decision against television has been a major key to the preservation of truth and holiness in the home. Spiritual men somehow saw the devastating long-term effects television would have on our society.

It is interesting that those who have stood against television for years, a decision which contributed significantly to preserving the church from liberal trends, have in recent years been joined by a spate of other concerned individuals in denouncing the pervasive influence of television. Those who have recently joined the resistance movement include religious people of various persuasions as well as the not-so-religious.

Many parents, professors, physicians, psychiatrists, sociologists, and even journalists have also joined against the effects of television. Numerous articles are in print such as "Give Up the Tube and Get Your Freedom," " 'Tube' Filling 'Booby Hatch,' " and "Tiny Superman Fans Making Fatal Dives" all denouncing the devastating effects of television. Many books have also been published such as *Rated X—The Moral Case Against TV, The Plug-In Drug, Four Reasons for the Elimination of Television,* and *Telegarbage.*

It is becoming increasingly common to read of educated, professional people, including those who make their living in some corner of the media, who either totally reject or severely limit television watching in their own homes. One example among many would be that of "The Incredible Hulk's" actor Bill Bixby. He refused to allow his four-year-old son to watch his own show. In explaining his ban on cartoons, Bixby said, "People think cartoons are harmless because they're not real. But children believe them."

Prophetic Foresight

Prophetic foresight is always vindicated in due

time. Who could have predicted the worldwide calamity which would spring from the union of the sons of God and the daughters of men but a "Noah"? Who could have visualized the smoky tendrils rising from the ruins of Sodom but an "Abraham"? Who but a "Daniel" could have predicted the disintegration of the mighty Babylonian empire?

How could a group of fundamental preachers predict the moral wasteland television would become? They could because they were led by the Spirit and because they knew scriptural principles. While there will always be inventors of things that will promote evil, and while we make no pretense that Scripture anticipates the technicalities of every future invention, basic scriptural principles cover every development which will ever be known to man.

Certain Things Are an Abomination to God

The essential nature of God is unchanging (Malachi 3:6). The things that pleased Him yesterday please Him today, and they will please Him tomorrow. Things that displeased Him yesterday displease Him today, and so will they tomorrow. That which displeases God does so because of its destructive nature. He desires for His children to have abundant life, and He knows that certain things are destructive and deadly. (See John 10:10.)

How are we to feel about those things which are an abomination to God? We must abhor, avoid, and take whatever steps are necessary to cut ourselves off from that which displeases the Lord. This separation causes us to refuse destructive elements a place in our home.

"Neither shalt thou bring an abomination into thine house, lest thou be a cursed thing like it: but thou shalt utterly detest it, and thou shalt utterly abhor it; for it is a cursed thing" (Deuteronomy 7:26). While the context of this verse of Scripture deals specifically with idols, the principle extends to anything that is an abomination.

It is forbidden to bring anything abominable into one's home. Why is this? It is because the abominable thing influences members of the family and corrupts them.

That which is abominable is cursed. Some things are blessed while others are cursed. When one associates with that which is blessed, or does things which are blessed, benefits accrue to him. But when he associates with or does that which is cursed, he opens the door to negative influences.

One's attitude toward an abomination should be utter hatred. When it is clearly determined that a thing or practice is an abomination, one's hatred of it should cause him to totally separate himself from it. His attitude will allow him to fulfill gladly the command of II Corinthians 6:17: "Wherefore come out from among them, and be ye separate, saith the Lord, and touch not the unclean thing; and I will receive you."

What does this have to do with television? Surely the metal, plastic, wood, or glass is not abominable! That is true. Neither is paper, ink, or glue abominable. The metal gears and rubber rollers of a printing press are not objectionable, nor is a camera and film. But any of these things can be used to produce abominations. It is not then the instruments that are abominable, but the evil products that men devise. It is not the television that is questionable, but the programming.

What things are abominable in the sight of God? A careful study of Scripture will reveal that there are at least six different categories of abominations.

Six Categories of Abominations

Moral abominations. These include all sexual sins and sins of the flesh, both inward and outward. God is morally pure and righteous, and He expects His children to be cleansed from all moral abominations. Some of the moral abominations God has warned us of include: incest (Leviticus 18:17), adultery and fornications (Ezekiel 18:1-13), sodomy (Leviticus 18:22), bestiality (Leviticus 18:23), transvestitism (Deuteronomy 22:5), whoredom (Deuteronomy 23:17-18), and a heart that devises wicked imaginations (Proverbs 6:16-18).

Occult Abominations. These include all types of idolatry which encourage the worship of objects, whether animate or inanimate, other than God. God condemns allowing children to be involved in false worship (Deuteronomy 18:9-14) and graven images (Deuteronomy 7:25). He does not condone divination, observing times, enchantment, or witchcraft. God also condemns charming, consulting with familiar spirits, wizardry, and necromancy (Deuteronomy 18:9-14).

Vocal abominations. These include numerous abuses of the human tongue. Our tongue was made to glorify God. Profaning God's name (Leviticus 18:21) is strictly disallowed. A lying tongue and a false witness are also condemned by God (Proverbs 6:16-19). He that sows discord (Proverbs 6:16-19) and justifies the wicked and condemns the just (Proverbs 17:15) are also abominations before God.

Violent abominations. These involve various attacks against the sacredness of human life. Some examples are hands that shed innocent blood (Proverbs 6:16-19), murder (Jeremiah 7:8-10), and robbing (Ezekiel 18:1-13).

Abominations of character. These concern the products of the inward man. A man's attitude governs his character and principle. If his character is corrupt, it may be revealed by dishonesty (Micah 6:9-16), following the example of the ungodly (Deuteronomy 12:29-32), or frowardness (rebellion)

(Proverbs 3:32).

A person lacking Christian character may have a proud look or feet swift to run to mischief (Proverbs 6:18), a desire to go the way of the wicked (Proverbs 15:8-9), or a proudness of heart (Proverbs 16:5). Stealing (Jeremiah 7:8-10), the oppression of others, involvement in iniquity, and false judgment are abominations which are often found in those who lack true character of the inward man. Such individuals also refuse to feed the hungry, refuse to clothe the naked and are guilty of taking increase. (See Ezekiel 18:1-13.)

Abominations of worship. These include such abominations as sacrificing to God less than the best (Deuteronomy 17:1), the sacrifices of a wicked person (Proverbs 15:8-9), and praying if one refuses to hear the Word of God (Proverbs 28:9).

The Negative Influence of Television

Are any of these abominations presented on television? Mary Lewis Coakley, in her book *Rated X— The Moral Case Against TV* (Arlington House, 1977), demonstrates that television is saturating "American homes with raw sex, blood and gore, slanted news, and subtle attacks on religion and morality, family and country." After sitting through hundreds of programs in preparation for her book, she assembled a table of contents which bears a striking resemblance to the list of scriptural abominations.

In *Christ and the Media,* Malcolm Muggeridge, veteran British journalist and broadcaster, announced his startling opinion that the media have "provided the Devil with perhaps the greatest opportunity accorded him since Adam and Eve were turned out of the Garden of Eden" (p. 15).

"If you want to know my absolutely candid opinion," Muggeridge said, "I think the best thing to do is not to look at television, and to that end, I have. . .disposed of my set" (p. 82).

The overwhelming majority of programming, nonetheless, falls into one of three major areas which correspond to the three root sins: greed, pride, and moral impurity. A glaring example of this is the fact that a youngster who watches television an average amount of time will have witnessed some 18,000 murders before he graduates from high school.

There can be no question that continued exposure to dramatized violence, immorality, and greed has a profound influence on the watcher. In commenting on the violent reaction of those who are continually exposed to violence on television, Marie Winn said, "Television conditions them to deal with real people as if they were on a television screen. Thus they are able to 'turn them off' quite simply, with a knife or a gun or a chain, with as little remorse as if they were turning off a television set" (*The Plug-In Drug,* Bantam Books, p. 84).

Television has such a powerful influence because it incorporates both the auditory and visual tracks of the brain. Reading a book allows the mind to produce the appropriate images, images which will be based on previous experience, personal values, and the written description. Television, however, supplies not only the words but the pictures. Reading stimulates creative imagination; TV suppresses it. The viewer sees what the producer wants him to see—no more and no less.

The person who watches television is, in effect, voluntarily subjecting himself to the mind-controlling and hypnotic influence of the tube. He has absolutely no input to the developments on the screen, and he exercises minimal effort to comprehend the message.

The eye is, to a large degree, the window of the soul. Jesus pointed this out when He said, "The light of the body is the eye: if therefore thine eye be single, thy whole body shall be full of light. But if thine eye be evil, thy whole body shall be full of darkness" (Matthew 6:22-23). Approximately one-third of what the world has to offer is "the lust of the eyes" (I John 2:16). Peter once described self-willed sinners as "having eyes full of adultery" (II Peter 2:14).

"I made a covenant with mine eyes," Job said, "why then should I think upon a maid?" (Job 31:1). Job wisely realized the influence of the eye-gate of the soul. He made a covenant with his eyes that he would not look at certain things. Since this was the case, and since the obvious result of looking is visual imagery, Job also recognized that consistency demanded that he not mentally conjure up wrong images.

God has given us the power of visualization and of creative imagination. Just as much as the hands, feet, or eyes, this ability is a member of our body and must be surrendered to Christ. "Neither yield ye your members as instruments of unrighteousness unto sin: but yield yourselves unto God, as those that are alive from the dead, and your members as instruments of righteousness unto God" (Romans 6:13).

Our struggle against evil is largely a battle of the mind: "(For the weapons of our warfare are not carnal, but mighty through God to the pulling down of strong holds;) Casting down imaginations, and every high thing that exalteth itself against the knowledge of God, and bringing into captivity every thought to the obedience of Christ" (II Corinthians 10:4-5). David realized this when he prayed, "Let the words of my mouth, and the meditation of my heart, be acceptable in thy sight, O LORD, my strength, and my redeemer" (Psalm 19:14).

"I will behave myself wisely in a perfect way. O when wilt thou come unto me? I will walk within my house with a perfect heart. I will set no wicked thing before mine eyes" (Psalm 101:2-3). He made further statements of commitment in the following verses:

- "I hate the work of them that turn aside" (verse 3).
- "A froward heart shall depart from me" (verse 4).
- "I will not know a wicked person" (verse 4).
- "Whoso privily slandereth his neighbour, him will I cut off" (verse 5).
- "Him that hath an high look and a proud heart will not I suffer" (verse 5).
- "He that worketh deceit shall not dwell within my house" (verse 7).
- "He that telleth lies shall not tarry in my sight" (verse 7).

If David were alive today, he would be unable to keep his commitment and have a television in his home since all of these things exist on television.

David realized the importance of not looking at wicked things. He also recognized the power of looking at right things (Psalm 101:6).

Victory Through Commitment

In view of God's hatred for abominable things, those who wish to please Him and live must make three basic commitments:

- To abstain personally from all abominations.
- To refuse to permit abominable persons to influence one's home.
- To cleanse the home of all abominations.

Such a commitment will result in the home being cleansed from questionable books, magazines, records, games, and trinkets. It will certainly result in the disposal of the television.

Such a cleansing process will be blessed of God, giving the Word of God the opportunity to take its rightful place of supremacy in the home. "And many that believed came, and confessed, and shewed their deeds. Many of them also which used curious arts brought their books together, and burned them before all men: and they counted the price of them, and found it fifty thousand pieces of silver. So mightily grew the word of God and prevailed" (Acts 19:18-20).

Those who stood against television in the early days of its invention were obviously led of God. Time has proven the destructive, deceptive use of the medium.

It has been demonstrated time and again that television has a negative effect on the morals, values, priorities, and learning abilities of the viewer. Contrary to the optimistic, early publicity for "children's educational programs," such efforts have not produced a generation of school children with advanced academic abilities.

We have also seen the disintegration of the once high standards of religious groups who permit the use of television in the home. Accompanying this loss is the decline of attendance at church services, as pastors find themselves competing on Sunday evening with the latest multimillion dollar Hollywood productions. Some churches abandoned Sunday evening services altogether, knowing they were fighting a losing battle.

Those whose pastors still stand faithfully against the evil influence of television should be grateful to God for giving prophetic foresight to men who have seen the devastating influence of TV. Only eternity will reveal how many homes have stayed together, how many children have been spared from losing their faith in God, and how many churches have prospered to win souls—all as a result of the decision to guard the window of the soul.

Test Your Knowledge

1. Statistics reveal that the average citizen spends about _____ years watching television.

2. It is not television itself which is questionable, but it is the _____.

3. Christians are not to yield their body members as instruments of _____, but rather they are to yield themselves unto _____.

4. The battle against evil is primarily a battle of the _____.

5. Realizing the importance of what he saw, David committed to set no _____ _____ before his eyes.

Try your hand at this word search
and see what is often displayed on T.V.

```
D F X V L S I G J E K B Y G N A M A N
P E P R G E C N E L O I V D M Z Q I W
S U I U W N O W O Q B X Q H K M G Q E
B B R J R A P E A G L T L R M C Z A W
T D J T C L E M I R C Y Y T K H D I G
V C M S N O I T A U T I S L A U X E S
O O E X G V H L O H O C L A Z J B B E
V X R P I D A I Y T I N A F O R P D G
M X V T S I E E H E M M T V X K I C M
N A U N R E I T D E E R G E P R Z A K
R N I S W M R A M T U W B L P C I T H
O S M H W O A S B Y T I L A R O M M I
A M U R D E R F I I C G B I Z H V X Y
G A D U L T E R Y D R E B E L L I O N
G U S P R U S M K X T O K W R P P N Q
```

65

Find These Hidden Words in the Puzzle on Preceding Page:

adultery	pride	drugs
profanity	crime	greed
murder	rebellion	sin
rape	disrespect	immorality
alcohol	sexual situations	violence

Apply Your Knowledge

Put yourself to the challenge that David did when he said, "I will set no wicked thing before mine eyes" (Psalm 101:3). Make a list of several worldly objects that you will refuse to look upon. You will find that each time you turn away from wicked sights God will honor your commitment and give you more strength.

Satan knows that one of the human's most vulnerable areas of weakness is in what he allows himself to see. If Satan can cause tempting sights to come before us, he can devise a careful plot against our soul through our sight.

As you resist evil sights, Satan will flee from you. You will find it true that the eyes are the windows of the soul.

Expand Your Knowledge

Read the beginning Scriptures for chapter six to prepare yourself for the chapter. These will lay a foundation of thought for you.

If you desire additional reading material you may try *Preserving the Pentecostal Lady* by Nell Morgan and Catherine Chambers or *In Search of Holiness* by David K. Bernard. Both are excellent and may be obtained from Word Aflame Press, 8855 Dunn Road, Hazelwood, Missouri 63042.

The Christian Appearance

In like manner also, that women adorn themselves in modest apparel, with shamefacedness and sobriety; not with broided hair, or gold, or pearls, or costly array.

I Timothy 2:9

Start With the Scriptures

Genesis 3:7-21	Isaiah 3:16-26; 61:10
Deuteronomy 22:5	I Peter 3:1-5
II Kings 9:30	Revelation 17:4-6

Our appearance is the manner in which we come before the world. It is what we display about our body and behavior. Appearance is the way we conduct ourselves and the way we wear our clothing.

The term "keep up appearances" is often used to denote a proper outward appearance. When our appearance enhances our Christian experience, there is no conflict with God's Word. But when the motive is to attract attention, we manifest pride. The ambition to appear unique and stand out from all others is a result of pride and will reveal impure motives in our fashion of dress. Our greatest concern should be for the reputation of Christ and the gospel rather than the building up of our own ego.

If one's motive is wrong, even the most commonplace clothing or mannerisms can give the appearance of pride. If his motive is right, a person can have very nice clothes and yet make a lovely appearance that displays gratitude rather than pride. The attitude with which we dress is as important as the clothes themselves for it will reveal our true spirit and motives in life.

It is said that Diogenes and Plato, two Greek philosophers who were contemporaries, had opposite ideas. Plato possessed some very beautiful carpets, and Diogenes felt that he would be more faithful to life and truth if he lived in poverty. One day Diogenes said some very disagreeable things in his ill-tempered way and jumped up and down on Plato's carpets. As he did, he said, "I trample on the pride of Plato!" Plato is said to have answered, "Yes, and with greater pride."

Either extreme is wrong. There can be just as much pride shown in an unkempt appearance as in the extreme adornment of the body.

The Christian should display himself in such a way that attention is drawn to Christ. The world needs a model in moral and spiritual living. They will only find this type of example in the lives of real Christians. True Christians reflect the light of Jesus Christ to this world.

Appearance in Wearing of Apparel

The word *apparel* comes from the Old French word *apareiller* which meant "to put like things together." The idea is one of clothing the body so that the garments enhance the individual. The clothes are not the main attraction, but they are the frame in which the most important object, the picture, is displayed. Clothes should be worn that will befit the person and reflect Christ.

It is obvious that God is concerned about the outward appearance of man. In the very beginning He intervened in man's attempt to clothe himself. The first man and woman tried fig leaves for clothing, but God did not feel that they were adequate. Fig leaves were not the frame which would enhance the glory of the man God had made in His image. Therefore, God gave them clothes made of the skins of animals.

From that time until now God has insisted that people wear clothing that adequately covers the body. Men often disagree about what is modest and what is not, but when God intervenes, the outcome will reflect modesty.

Many people have observed that before God came into their lives, they were not conscious of their improper clothing. But when the Spirit brought conviction, they suddenly felt ashamed at the exposure of their bodies.

God has always set the proper example for our clothing. God is a Spirit and could appear to us in any form He desires. Yet when He appeared as a man, He dressed in clothes which expressed His glory. (See Revelation 1:13; 3:5; 4:4; 7:9; 15:6; 19:14.) In His appearances, attention was quickly transferred from His clothes to Himself. His clothes were appropriate. They served as a frame for His presence as a picture frame enhances the painting. They were not so elaborate as to be awesome, yet they were rich enough that they spoke of His deity.

God has often shown much concern about the way His children were adorned. Mention has been made of His intervention in the way Adam and Eve were clothed (Genesis 3:21). He had Joshua the High Priest change from his filthy clothes (Zechariah

3:3-5). When He left the demoniac, the man was clothed and in his right mind (Mark 5:15). God placed in His Law the requirement for a distinction between male and female in the clothes they wore (Deuteronomy 22:5).

God was very concerned about the way His priests appeared before the people. He wanted them to dress appropriately for the dignity of their office. He caused them to wear garments which were "for glory and for beauty" (Exodus 28:2). Those who drew near to God were to appear neatly dressed and attractive. The clothes they wore were exemplary of their dignity and position. The attractiveness of their clothing was not gaudy as to draw attention to the person. Instead, they wore clothes that spoke of the God they served and represented in this world.

If clothes do not say something about the inner man, they are not adequate. The priests of idol worshipers were often dressed in gaudy, flashy, and sensual clothing that purposely drew attention to themselves. These detracted from the supposedly religious exercises they performed by drawing personal attention.

Clothes should not expose the body but rather hide our shame and nakedness. To be unclothed or exposed has always been a cause of shame. Moses drew a line and called those who would to come over on the Lord's side when he found Aaron had made Israel "naked unto their shame among their enemies" (Exodus 32:25). God pled with the church of Laodicea to clothe themselves with His garments of righteousness that the shame of their nakedness would not appear (Revelation 3:18). In showing the need for a new resurrection body, Paul used the analogy of putting on clothes, "that being clothed we shall not be found naked" (II Corinthians 5:3).

As soon as Adam and Eve committed the first sin in the Garden of Eden, they knew that they were naked; and when they knew it, they were uneasy with each other. They were both embarrassed and felt indecent. This is the story of the first blush, first guilt,.and the first feeling of shame.

From that day until now, nakedness has been shameful. There are some whose conscience seems no longer to bother them when their bodies are exposed, but it is certainly not a normal experience.

A person who has a healthy state of mind does not desire to expose his body. Yet it was not unusual that the demoniac who lived in the tombs was unclothed. When Jesus came to him, he was soon "clothed, and in his right mind" (Mark 5:15). The fact that being properly clothed and being in one's right mind are complementary terms is rather obvious from this passage. It would also appear that the closer to satanic control a person becomes, the further he would be from being in his right mind. His clothing or lack of clothing could possibly reflect that distance. As long as this man had been demon possessed among the tombs, he felt no embarrassment or shame. But when he came into contact with Jesus and regained his right mind, his exposed body became intolerable.

As we grow in Christ, He continually guides our convictions concerning our appearance.

It is an abomination for a woman to wear men's clothing or for a man to wear women's clothing (Deuteronomy 22:5). This is a scriptural principle that does not change. Things that were an abomination to God in the past will continue to be an abomination. He is God and He changes not (Malachi 3:6). When God created the man and woman, He designed them to be distinctly different and to fulfill their respective roles. God continues to expect that distinction of separation between the male and female.

Some have observed that there are other verses

in Deuteronomy twenty-two which require things we do not abide by today. They point out that if it is wrong to wear clothing of the opposite sex, it is also wrong to plant two crops in the same field or wear a suit with linen and wool combined.

This argument falls short because of a particular truth. The principle of the law has never been changed. Although we no longer use certain ceremonies, the principle behind every law of God forever remains the same. We no longer offer animal sacrifices, but the truth remains that there is no redemption without the shedding of blood, and only Jesus' blood atones for sin. A leper is no longer sent to the priest, but the principle of separation from that which is unclean has not changed. The loss of the ceremony did not change the principle behind it.

Jesus came and condemned sin in the flesh "that the righteousness of the law might be fulfilled in us" (Romans 8:4). Although the Law was weak and could not accomplish what Christ did through His sacrifice, every principle in the Law is still valid. The statement "Thou shalt not make unto thee any graven image" (Exodus 20:4) is under that same Law. The same argument could be used for making an idol today.

Although certain requirements of ceremony are no longer binding where the principle is not violated, where that principle would be violated it is wrong to do that thing. Thus it is still wrong to make an idol, and it is still wrong to wear clothing of the opposite sex.

The principle remains that God wants a separation and distinction between the sexes. He does not want defilement which He taught with the requirement of oxen and donkeys not plowing together and with the law of not wearing clothes made of linen and wool mixed. When He said there was to be no wearing of clothing which pertained to the opposite sex, there was also a very vital and obvious principle involved that must not be violated.

God does not want men to appear as women, or women to appear as men. There must be a definite distinction. The more a person endeavors to appear like the opposite sex, the more abominable it is to God. That principle does not change.

It is obvious that slacks make a woman look more like a man than a woman in the same way that a dress would cause a man to appear feminine. Even if he arranged the dress to look different from that worn by most women, it would still look like a woman's garment. It would be obvious to others that the man had on a woman's garment even if he altered it and made it of blue denim or leather. It would be the same situation with a woman wearing slacks. It is no more possible to have such a thing as women's slacks as it would be to have a man's dress. This is due to the normal, natural distinction God placed between the sexes.

Appearance in Conduct of Life

The Apostle Paul said that we are to abstain from the very appearance of evil (I Thessalonians 5:22). One may despise drunkenness, but if he is seen around bars and taverns others will judge him to be a drunkard because of his appearance.

The psalmist said that those who delight in the law of the Lord are not seen standing around with sinners (Psalm 1:1). When those who scorn are sitting in their seats of criticism, the one who delights in the law of the Lord is somewhere meditating on God's Word. When Jesus was with sinners, it was always with the purpose of leading them to truth. He did not keep their company to enjoy their sinful ways nor to condemn them, but rather to lead them to salvation. He was an influence to them instead of allowing them to influence Him.

Jesus also condemned the appearance of men who appear to be more religious than they are. When we pray, fast, and give alms, it should be with the proper motive and in the right spirit. When we appear to men to fast (Matthew 6:16), or pray to be heard (Matthew 6:5), or give our alms to be seen of men (Matthew 6:2), we lose our reward.

One must be careful at all times to give the proper appearance. A man might be tempted to display a double standard. He could be tempted to behave differently when away from home from the way he would at home. Some might feel that once they get away from home, it is permissable to go swimming at the beach or other public places where there are mixed bathers. Because they are unknown, they have the tendency to justify their deeds.

Jesus said that it was adulterous for a man to look upon a woman with lust. By that same reasoning, it would be adulterous for a person to so expose his body that others would be caused to lust after him. If a person is causing an adulterous situation, it does not matter whether he is known or not. For that reason mixed bathing is an undesirable activity for the Christian regardless of where he may be.

The Bible clearly expresses the need for modesty in both apparel and behavior (I Peter 3:1-5; I Timothy 2:8-10). Christians should behave themselves circumspectly with sobriety and shamefacedness. A Christian woman will not desire to dress in such a way as to allure men to desire her in a sensual relationship. Neither should the Christian male dress to be "macho" and exude great sexual appeal.

Both the man and woman should be virtuous in every aspect of their lives. The true lady will present herself so that she wins respect and pleases God rather than men. The gentleman will want to do the same. Both should desire to emanate the presence of Jesus Christ to the world by their Christian behavior.

Appearance in Physical Expressions

The Apostle Peter used the words *outward adorning* to describe the kind of adornment that women should not employ. The Greek word he used was *kosmos,* from which we get our word *cosmetics.* Peter said that the woman's cosmetics were to be the hidden character of the heart.

Changing the facial features with cosmetics and dyeing the hair are methods some use to try to hide their real self. Martin Luther said, "A woman should be thus disposed as not to care for adornment. Else when people turn their minds to adornment, they never give it up; that is their way and their nature." The pride of one's heart causes a person to want to hide the way God made them. Instead of being ashamed of the way God made our features, we should be grateful that we are unique.

A lady once came to John Newton curious about the best rule of conduct in dress. He told her, "Madam, so dress and so conduct yourself that persons who have been in your company will not recollect what you had on."

What effect does jewelry have on people? It draws attention to the affluence and the glory of the person wearing it. It is a symbol of the possessions of man, not God. It is a symbol of the glory of man, not God.

Jewelry symbolizes the pride of a man's life. Jewelry is an ego-builder and a means for drawing the envious eye to the person who wears it. Every reason for which a man would wear jewelry is indicative of the pride of life. It does not glorify God. In fact, it distracts from God's glory.

The same is true of the coloring of one's hair, which is another effort to camouflage the real person. It diverts attention from that which is important to a fictitious parade of self.

It was God who said, "Man looketh on the outward appearance" (I Samuel 16:7). God was revealing His own ability to see what was inside the man. But the converse of that was that man can only judge by the outward appearance. There are only three things we see in observing others: their clothing, conduct, and physical expressions.

Once he has looked on the outward appearance, a person makes a value judgment of that which he sees. Thus all people express their character in these three ways.

A man dresses to express his station in life. Clothes distinguish a person for that which he is publicly. He frequents places which manifest his lifestyle. Through his daily behavior he expresses his values and philosophy of life. Finally, he shows in his every gesture what he really is inside.

Test Your Knowledge

1. What causes some people to desire to appear unique and different from all others?

2. The Christian should dress in such a way as to draw attention to whom?

3. What was the first mention in the Bible of God intervening in the way men dressed?

4. God wanted high priests to dress appropriately for their _____ and _____.

5. To be unclothed or naked has always been a cause of _____.

6. According to Deuteronomy 22:5, God expects a _____ between the way a man and a woman dresses.

7. Apostle Peter said that a woman's adorning should be that of the _____.

8. What effects does jewelry have on individuals? List at least three. _____

_____

9. Man looks on the outward _____,

but God looks on the _____.

10. Since man does look on the outward appearance of others it is important that a Christian guard three areas of his appearance. List these three areas. _____

_____

Apply Your Knowledge

Here is a challenging idea that may prove to have interesting results.

People often ask Christians, "Are you a Christian?" There is something about a Christian that seems to send signals to those he comes in contact with. There is a certain feeling that others have that causes them to sense one's association with Jesus Christ.

Keep a small notepad or diary with you. The next time someone senses that you are a Christian and asks you, simply question them as to why they felt you were. At a convenient time make a few notes of your discovery.

You may want to continue this for several months and see what happens. At a later date compare all of your findings. This experience may reveal to you even more forcibly the things that people observe about Christians, and it should serve as an encouragement to maintain a "Christian appearance" at all times.

Expand Your Knowledge

Read *Start With the Scriptures* for the next chapter to better acquaint yourself with the material. Look up and list as many verses of Scripture as you can relating to wine or strong drink in the Bible. Having read them, decide for yourself how God feels about drinking alcoholic beverages. The Bible leaves no question as to God's desire for His people concerning the maintenance of their bodies.

A Clean Temple

Let not sin therefore reign in your mortal body, that ye should obey it in the lusts thereof.

Romans 6:12

Start With the Scriptures

Proverbs 23:21-33
Isaiah 5:11; 28:7
Mark 7:20-23
Luke 21:34

Romans 6
II Corinthians 6:14-18; 7:1
Galatians 5:21

God cares greatly for those things which are reserved for His purposes. Because of their sanctified purpose He will not tolerate their abuse.

A considerable portion of the first five books of the Bible contains explicit instructions concerning the proper use of the Tabernacle. Only the priests could enter the Holy Place, and only then after a cleansing at the laver in the courtyard. The Holy of Holies could be entered only by the high priest, and that but once a year on the Day of Atonement. The priests had to be appropriately dressed and consecrated, and their behavior while in service had to conform to specifically prescribed standards.

When the Philistines took possession of the Ark of the Covenant, they found themselves continually plagued with unusual and deadly diseases. When Uzzah touched the Ark, he fell dead. As Belshazzar drank from the holy vessels he sealed his fate, and the disembodied hand wrote it on the wall for all to see.

All these facts serve as examples of the truth that God will not allow the abuse of holy things. "Know ye not that ye are the temple of God, and that the Spirit of God dwelleth in you? If any man defile the temple of God, him shall God destroy; for the temple of God is holy, which temple ye are" (I Corinthians 3:16-17).

Temple of the Holy Ghost

Specifically, it is your body which is the temple of the Holy Ghost. We should glorify God in our bodies and in our spirits which belong to God and are reserved for His holy purposes. (See I Corinthians 6:19-20.) This truth is so serious with God that He promised to destroy any who defile His temple.

Every sincere Christian should ask himself, "In what ways is it possible to defile my body? What steps of action can I take to purify the temple?"

Is defiling the temple purely a spiritual matter, or is it possible for the temple to be defiled by physical actions?

The scope of the Apostle Paul's words in I Corinthians six is that the temple is defiled by moral impurity. While the root of moral impurity is a spiritual matter, it is ultimately expressed by the body. Paul said that a person who commits fornication with a harlot becomes one flesh with the harlot. (See I Corinthians 6:15-20.) The principle is that while the beginning of defilement is in the spirit, its final manifestation will be in the flesh. There is filthiness of both the flesh and the spirit, and we are to cleanse ourselves from both (II Corinthians 7:1).

What should be the attitude of the Christian toward fleshly sins which include drinking, smoking, and drug abuse? Are these purely physical matters, or do spiritual sins give birth to them? (See Mark 7:20-23.)

It is clear from Scripture that sin must have a body through which to express itself. This occurs as the members of the body are yielded to sinful practices. Paul admonished the Romans concerning this truth. "Let not sin therefore reign in your mortal body, that ye should obey it in the lusts thereof. Neither yield ye your members as instruments of unrighteousness unto sin: but yield yourselves unto God, as those that are alive from the dead, and your members as instruments of righteousness unto God. . .Know ye not, that to whom ye yield yourselves servants to obey, his servants ye are to whom ye obey; whether of sin unto death, or of obedience unto righteousness?" (Romans 6:12-13, 16).

It is, then, possible to sin with the body. Sinning is not just a matter of wrong attitudes or thoughts, although it includes these. Sin can be accomplished with the eyes, ears, hands, feet, mind, mouth, or any other member of the body. Jesus recognized the devastating effects of sins accomplished by body members and boldly announced that it would be better to be deprived of a hand, a foot or an eye than to suffer the eternal fires of hell (Mark 9:43-48).

Christians should examine their physical habits to be certain they are not engaging in sinful practices. Since it is possible to sin with the body, and since the body of the believer is the temple of God, we must cleanse ourselves from the filthiness of the flesh according to God's command.

Drinking

"Wine is a mocker, strong drink is raging: and whosoever is deceived thereby is not wise" (Proverbs 20:1).

There are three categories of references to wine or drinking in Scripture.

- Where wine is mentioned, but neither endorsed nor condemned.
- Where wine is identified as a source of misery and as an emblem of the wrath of God.
- Where wine is identified as a blessing in conjunction with corn and bread.

Some religious movements today permit or even encourage the use of intoxicants in moderation. A careful examination of Scripture will reveal, however, that alcoholic beverages are never spoken of favorably and that partaking of such beverages in any quantity is harmful to the human body. Intoxicants poison or fill the body with toxins. The intentional poisoning of our body is abusive of the temple of God. For these reasons, drinking is certainly a sinful practice in God's eye.

Those references to wine which fall under the first category previously mentioned cannot be appealed to in support of drinking. Scripture often mentions practices without condemning or endorsing them, purely as a part of a larger context of describing human actions.

The references in the second category clearly condemn the use of wine in any quantity. One of these denunciations of wine was written by Solomon, who had been blessed of God with great wisdom. He wrote, "Who hath woe? who hath sorrow? who hath contentions? who hath babbling? who hath wounds without cause? who hath redness of eyes? They that tarry long at the wine; they that go to seek mixed wine. Look not thou upon the wine when it is red, when it giveth his colour in the cup, when it moveth itself aright. At the last it biteth like a serpent, and stingeth like an adder. Thine eyes shall behold strange women, and thine heart shall utter perverse things. Yea, thou shalt be as he that lieth down in the midst of the sea, or as he that lieth upon the top of a mast. They have stricken me, shalt thou say, and I was not sick; they have beaten me, and I felt it not: when shall I awake? I will seek it yet again'' (Proverbs 23:29-35).

This passage graphically describes the evils of drinking intoxicating beverages. The sure result is sorrow, woe, contention, senseless talk, and wounds. Drinking produces no good result. It breaks down moral restraints and causes a person to say things he would never say otherwise. A person who drinks is in danger of immediate death due to the effects of intoxication, not to mention the long-term, addictive results of alcohol.

"Woe unto them that rise up early in the morning, that they may follow strong drink; that continue until night, till wine inflame them!'' (Isaiah 5:11). "But they also have erred through wine, and through strong drink are out of the way; the priest and the prophet have erred through strong drink, they are swallowed up of wine, they are out of the way through strong drink; they err in vision, they stumble in judgment'' (Isaiah 28:7). These verses show the addictive nature of intoxicating beverages and the fact that those who partake of them will err in matters of judgment; their senses are polluted.

It is the third category of references which prompts some to excuse alcoholic beverages, often with the hopeful intention to drink in moderation. There is no way to know how many have fallen into the treacherous trap of drunkenness by prefacing their tippling with, "After all, didn't Paul tell Timothy to take a little wine for his stomach's sake?''

There are two kinds of wines mentioned in Scripture. As William Patton said in *Bible Wines or Laws of Fermentation And Wines of the Ancient* (reprinted by Sane Press), "There were. . .two kinds of wine in ancient use. The one was sweet, pleasant, refreshing, unfermented; the other was exciting, inflaming, intoxicating. Each was called wine" (p. 132).

Patton meticulously documents the fact that unfermented beverages, called wines, existed and were commonly used by the ancients. He gives abundant proof of the generic nature of the two Hebrew words, *yayin* and *shakar* (pp. 56-58).

- *Yayin* (translated "wine") "designates grape-juice, or the liquid which the fruit of the vine yields. This may be new or old, sweet or sour, fermented or unfermented, intoxicating or unintoxicating" (p. 56).
- *Shakar* (translated "strong drink") " 'signifies "sweet drink" expressed from fruits other than the grape, and drunk in an unfermented or fermented state' " (pp. 57, 58).

These two words are generic. In other words, they are used in Scripture to refer both to fermented and unfermented drink. The context determines which meaning is meant.

There are other relevant Hebrew words which always carry the same meaning. One of the most common is *tirosh,* (translated "wine," "new wine," and "sweet wine"): this "wine" is an unfermented drink which generally refers to the juice of something other than the grape; for example, corn and olives.

The New Testament makes use of a generic Greek word, *oinos,* to correspond exactly to *yayin* in the Old Testament. It too designates the juice of the grape in all its stages. The context will determine whether fermented or unfermented beverage is meant.

The English word *wine* is from the Latin *vinum,* which is equivalent to the Greek *oinos. Vinus* is a generic word which refers to the juice of the grape in all its forms, as was the English *wine* during the era of the translation of the Authorized Version. More recent dictionaries will define *wine* exclusively as a fermented beverage, but we must be careful not to allow modern day usage of a word to be retroactive.

The reason for the development of the restricted meaning of wine to fermented liquid only is described by John Stuart Mill in his *System of Logic:* "A generic term is always liable to become limited to a single species if people have occasion to think and speak of that species oftener than of anything else contained in the genus. The tide of custom first drifts the word on the shore of a particular meaning, then retires and leaves it there." (Quoted by Patton on pp. 63-64.)

What did Paul mean when he said to Timothy, "Drink no longer water, but use a little wine for thy stomach's sake and thine often infirmities" (I Timothy 5:23). Did he command Timothy to indulge in fermented alcoholic beverages for the sake of a weak stomach? Such would seem to be precisely the wrong prescription if fermented wine was intended. Indeed, the fermented wines of that day produced "headaches, dropsy, madness, and stomach complaints" (Patton, p. 112). At the same time there were unfermented wines which were "exceedingly wholesome and useful to the body" (Patton, p. 113).

Surely Paul, who had earlier told Timothy that a bishop must not be given to wine (I Timothy 3:3), and who knew the inherent evil of fermented wine from the law ("wine is a mocker"), would not have recommended to Timothy such a forbidden, dangerous substance to drink in the place of water.

Some make their plea for moderate use of alcohol on the basis of a misunderstanding of Ephesians 5:18: "And be not drunk with wine, wherein is excess. . . ." They point out that one is not to drink to excess, or until he is drunk.

The literal meaning of the Greek word translated *excess* is, however, "dissolution, dissipation." In this case the word *excess* does not refer to quantity, but to that which is inherent in fermented wine. The phrase, "wherein is," reveals that the "excess" is *in the wine*. In other words, the use of fermented wine dissipates.

It has also been pointed out by physicians that the first drink of alcohol intoxicates. After that, the drunkenness is only a matter of degree.

Twenty-five percent of the American people are directly affected by alcoholism. Ninety percent of college students and seventy percent of high school students drink. These amazing statistics contributed to nearly 22,000 alcohol related deaths in one recent year among those in the fifteen to twenty-four age group. (Statistics from *Christian School Comment,* Vol. 12, No. 9.)

The only consistent Christian position is total abstinence from all alcoholic beverages. Moderation is the first step toward immoderation. The person who refuses to drink will never have to concern himself with fears of drinking too much. He will never be tempted to drunkenness, or in the more polite term of our society, alcoholism. He will live his life free from the ravages of liquor.

Smoking

It is a highly documented fact that smoking contributes to cancer of the lungs, mouth, and lips. So convincing is the evidence that the Surgeon General of the United States won the fight to have a warning placed on every package of cigarettes and every advertisement for cigarettes.

Tobacco is a habit-forming narcotic. Among unbiased researchers, there is no question as to the devastating effect of smoking on the human body.

Many godly men stood against the use of tobacco for years before medical research determined its danger. How did they have the foresight to avoid this dangerous practice?

While there is no verse which says, "Thou shalt not smoke," there are many verses of Scripture which teach a Christian to resist coming under the power of any substance. A Christian should even resist falling under the power of lawful practices. Paul said, "All things are lawful for me, but I will not be brought under the power of any" (I Corinthians 6:12). "Put a knife to thy throat," Solomon warned, "if thou be a man given to appetite" (Proverbs 23:2).

There is no question that tobacco defiles the body, which is the temple of God. It coats the lungs with tar, promotes various ailments including cancer, and robs the smoker of vitality, alertness, and years of life.

Would God have approved of a vandal entering His Holy of Holies in the Tabernacle and painting the Ark of the Covenant with a tar brush? Of course not. Neither can He approve of His children defiling the temple of the body. God will surely judge those who defile His temple.

Drugs

In many ways, all that has previously been said about alcohol and tobacco applies equally to the abuse of drugs.

There is, however, a scripturally endorsed use of medicine. (See Proverbs 17:22.) Jesus recognized the value of physicians to the sick (Matthew 9:12). Luke continued to be referred to as "the beloved physician'' long after his conversion (Colossians 4:14).

It is wrong, of course, to trust solely in physicians or medicines. One's trust must be in the Lord and He must be recognized as the source of all healing.

Many question the wisdom of the philosophy of the modern medical profession toward drugs. Ethical dilemmas may present themselves, specifically related to the frequent prescription of placebos. In fact, Dr. Sissela Bock has said that half of all prescriptions written are for placebos.

Doctors debate the ethics of charging the high prices for placebos which are demanded for drugs, but others point out that if the placebos were sold for their actual value, the patient would immediately suspect that his prescription was not real medicine and would thus have no confidence in it.

But aside from the questions of drug use as related to the medical profession, today we face the epidemic of drug abuse by people of all ages. The problem ranges from those who smoke marijuana to the Valium addicts.

A Christian must not allow himself to come under the power of any habit-forming drug. It has been documented repeatedly in volumes of scientific and medical reports that drug abuse is a deadly pursuit. The only individuals who question these findings are those who for personal gain or pleasure wish to excuse the abuse of drugs. They might insist that some great, mysterious conspiracy exists to keep them from experiencing the harmless pleasures of drugs.

But where are the healthy drug addicts? There are none. As has been witnessed repeatedly in the rock music scene, drugs kill mercilessly those who have done the most to popularize their use.

The word that is translated ''witchcraft'' or ''sorcery'' in our English Bible is *pharmakeia,* the same word from which we get ''pharmacy.'' It implies the abuse of drugs to induce altered stages of consciousness to aid in occultic practices. It is listed with the works of the flesh in Galatians 5:20, and it is one of the things which will bar one from the kingdom of God.

What effect does drug abuse have on our society?

- More than half the deaths on American highways are alcohol or drug related.
- More than half the crashes in small non-commercial aircraft are caused by alcohol or drugs.
- Eighty-five percent of physical child abuse in America is caused by parents who are "stoned out of their minds" [*Christian School Comment*, Vol. 12, No. 9).

There is no justification for the use of drugs by Christians. It is a mind-altering, violence-producing, habit-forming, disease-developing practice which must be shunned as yet another satanic attempt to defile the temple of God.

Drinking, smoking, and drug abuse are not the only ways in which a Christian can defile the holy temple of his body. But these are three of the most common and visible ways, and they must be shunned at any cost. The Christian who stands for total abstinence from alcohol, tobacco, and drugs will shine as a bright light in a dark, corrupt world.

Test Your Knowledge

True or False

_____1. In the Old Testament, there were several accounts of people who were struck dead by God for abusing holy things.

_____2. I Corinthians 3:16-17 indicates that God is more tolerant now and will tolerate men abusing the holy temple of God.

_____3. The body can be defiled by physical actions as well as spiritual actions.

_____4. It is sometimes permissible for a Christian to allow sin in his mortal being. (See Romans 6:12-13, 16.)

_____5. Intoxicants actually poison the body.

_____6. The results of drinking alcoholic beverages include sorrow, woe, contentions, senseless talk, and wounds.

_____7. Although the Scriptures forbid drinking, they permit one to look upon the drinks.

_____8. All wine in Bible times was fermented.

_____9. Tobacco is a habit-forming narcotic.

_____10. A Christian should not come under the influence of any habit-forming drug.

Apply Your Knowledge

How many people are really happy about their use of alcohol, tobacco, or drugs? The answer is probably very few. Self-esteem, attitudes, and general well-being all increase remarkably when one leaves such vices behind and experiences real deliverance.

Try to obtain some testimonies to see how others have felt when delivered from one or all of these harmful habits. Some outstanding testimonies of deliverance from alcohol can be obtained from: Spirit of Freedom, P. O. Box 50583, New Orleans, Louisiana 70150.

Expand Your Knowledge

Prepare for chapter eight, by reading the Scriptures listed under *Start With the Scriptures*. This will lay the foundation for the chapter before you actually begin to study it.

It would be edifying for you to list all the recreational activities you participate in. After listing them, list all the good and bad points about each one. As you then read chapter eight you will more easily be able to let the Spirit guide you to evaluate the value of your activities as a Christian.

Worldly Amusements

8

Dearly beloved, I beseech you as strangers and pilgrims, abstain from fleshly lusts, which war against the soul.

I Peter 2:11

Start With the Scriptures

Ecclesiastes 3:1-8
Romans 14:19-23
Galatians 5:17-26
Ephesians 2:2
I John 2:15

II Timothy 3:1-5
Titus 2:12
James 1:14-15
II Peter 2:13

Men often desire to be entertained by something or someone. It seems that boredom develops if something is not constantly happening. Men sometimes wander from one place of entertainment to another, looking for constant changes and new thrills. The problem with such searching is that amusements often lose their thrill. Restraints are often thrown aside as one endeavors to obtain the same satisfaction he once knew. It becomes a hopelessly vicious circle of total disillusionment.

Recreational Needs

The human body needs a certain amount of relaxation and recreation. Although the Apostle Paul relegated bodily exercise to a lower level than spiritual exercise, bodily exercise does profit a little (I Timothy 4:8).

It is generally agreed that every man has his diversion from toil. Some might be tempted to condemn the way another man spends his free time while he himself seeks other means of enjoyment.

Jesus once told His disciples to come apart to rest (Mark 6:31). He knew that feelings can become numb and the productivity of life decrease under the continual pressure of toil. It is similar to the reaction of one's hand when he holds on to something tightly. The constant pressure soon causes the feelings to deaden. For this reason Jesus recognized the proper place of rest and recreation.

It is good to enjoy times of informal fellowship with other Christians. This is one reason God instituted many feast days in the Old Testament. The feasts were times of eating and rejoicing in leisure.

There are many ways that Christians can enjoy fellowship with each other. There are picnics, games, singspirations, and sightseeing excursions. There are also such things as museums and industries to visit, as well as historical points and sights of nature. There are numerous ways for the Christian to enjoy himself.

Many people would like a catalog of things which they can and cannot do, as though the sinfulness lies within the particular game or event. However, the problem may not lie in the activity as much as in the spirit of that event. A good thing can be harmful if indulged in at the wrong time (Ecclesiastes 3:1) or too often. The atmosphere and climate of certain activities must be considered.

The environment of some forms of recreation automatically eliminates the Christian from participation. This is the reason why Christians should not frequent the bowling alley or pool hall. The worldly atmosphere of bowling alleys, skating rinks, or pool halls is not conducive to godly living. Although there is nothing inherently evil within many of these activities, such communion with the world is not for the child of God.

Music affects the moods and spirit of a man. The Christian should be sure the music he listens to uplifts the soul. There is no legitimate reason to listen to rock music or other worldly songs. The music one listens to can greatly affect his spirit and attitude.

Every recreational exercise should pass the test of having some redeemable value. It should provide wholesome fellowship or have an educational purpose. It should at least be free of any shade of evil appearance (I Thessalonians 5:22), while offering the participant recreation and exercise.

Christian recreation should certainly not detract from our spiritual relationship with God. It would be foolish for us to participate in that which would eventually harm us spiritually.

Sometimes a sin is something good which has become abused. Eating, for instance, can be made into a sin even though it is a necessary activity. God slew thousands of Israelites for eating quail because of the spirit in which they ate it and their obsession for it. The attitude of the Israelites in lusting after flesh showed their carnality. Is it sinful to eat quail? Certainly not! But God weighs the spirits and actions of men (I Samuel 2:3). When we make something an obsession (Proverbs 23:2), it becomes sinful.

Christians should exercise great care when playing games which invite intense competition. It would be a good idea for some of the more mature participants to share the responsibility of supervising the games. If only one person allows his carnal nature to get out of control, the entire game can be spoiled with emulation, anger, and resentment. Such feelings ruin the entire purpose for recreation.

This is the reason why Christians should not compete with the world. The world's objective is to satisfy the flesh to its fullest. Christian entertainment is not for that purpose. The Christian's objectives simply do not mix with the goals of those who are yet carnal. Since sinners soon become sated with their pleasures in the world, they must replace the old activities with new or more exciting ones. Their pleasures are without concern to godly principles, but the Christian seeks to please God in all things.

For the child of God, physical pleasures to satisfy recreational and physical needs must rise above carnality and sin. They must be more subdued and allow the Holy Spirit to remain active and not be grieved in our lives. We must keep the old nature submitted to the spiritual nature. We should not indulge in any pleasure which might hinder our walk with God.

If a seemingly harmless game would cause a person to become worldly minded, it should be avoided. Gambling and games of chance lead to, and may be produced by, greed, envy and covetousness. These are serious sins that a Christian cannot afford in his heart. Ball games can lead to hatred and slander against fellow Christians if participants fail to maintain the proper spirit. Any sport or recreation which does not build a Christian spirit is wrong.

Recreation should never become a way of life. It should be a reward for labor. It ought to be a diversion rather than an obsession.

The Climate of Sin

There is a strong tendency for the flesh to overrule our spirituality. Our natural tendencies endeavor to influence our actions more than our spiritual tendencies. This is why we must abstain from any fleshly lust which will war against the soul (I Peter 2:11). To abstain means to hold one's self off from or to keep away.

Fleshly lusts are carnal desires which satisfy the natural man. These desires result from an evaluation of the possessions and evils of this life. Jesus said that lust has a highly destructive power that will choke out the Word of God (Mark 4:19). The Apostle Paul spoke of lust as being the driving power in man's flesh. The flesh is the sinful nature which has turned from God and cannot be reconciled to God (Romans 8:7). If we walk in the Spirit, however, we will not fulfill the lust of the flesh (Galatians 5:16).

Epithymia, the Greek word for lust or desire, means to seek gratification. "It urges man to activity. When all is said and done, it expresses the deeply rooted tendency in man to find the focus of his life in himself, to trust himself, to love himself more than others. Paul equates this tendency with the flesh and the passions (Ephesians 2:3), the powers which draw a man away from God. The power of the 'old nature' (Ephesians 4:22) is seen in *epithymia.*" *(The New International Dictionary of New Testament Theology.* Vol. 1, p. 457.)

The atmosphere created by some amusements caters to the lusts of the carnal man. For this reason, we should carefully examine anything we do for pleasure.

By the late Greek classical period, pleasure had come to mean "man's involvement in his material surroundings, which held down the soul trying to mount up to God. It was considered that the one who let himself be ruled by *hedone* (pleasure) had missed the purpose of life." *(The New International Dictionary of Testament Theology,* Vol. 1, p. 459.)

Paul said that there was a time when we served various lusts and pleasures before Jesus saved us (Titus 3:3). Peter spoke of those who were given over to rioting or revelling in times past (I Peter 4:2-4).

The Christian must be careful that his amusements do not create a climate in which sin can be produced. Rock music creates this type of climate. It builds up the physical emotions above the spiritual. The beat of the music affects the body while the melody influences the inner man. When the physical elements rise above the spiritual, there is created a climate for sensuality. Since rock music is conducive to the carnal nature, it is not surprising that witchcraft, drugs, and promiscuity are products of its culture.

People are not interested in God on the dance floor. The dimly-lit halls do not provide the climate which is conducive to discussing Scripture. The atmosphere of such places does not invite holiness. Dancing has always carried a sexual overtone. Only when a person was dancing before the Lord was it a holy action (II Samuel 6:14). It was an act of worship to God which employed no partner and was unctioned by God's Spirit. The modern amusement of dancing to music is not unto the Lord, nor is it holy. It is carnal and sensuous and should be denounced by the true child of God.

Worldly amusements lack any reference to God. Instinctively, there is an incongruity between worldly entertainments and God. Even when they begin with a mixture of religion, the religious subject is soon dropped, and the secular takes its place. The natural history of many amusements has been one away from God. In the Scriptures, references to man's pleasure are almost invariably shown in a bad light. When a person is in a situation or place where he is uncomfortable, he is probably in the wrong place.

In previous years religious people felt that the healthiest pattern for men was to stay busy, bent on some great ideal, so that they did not need to be amused. Today, however, people have more leisure time than ever before. There is often a feeling that this extra time must be used for enjoyment because it is earned.

A philosophy of all play and no responsibility can be the possible result of such a generation. If one lives by this philosophy, he should at least make sure that leisure time is spent in a wholesome manner. Television and other such entertainment are not the kinds of wholesome activities in which the Christian should be engaged. Anything which distracts one from Christian service is unwholesome. Anything which compromises Christian convictions or creates a climate of sin should be considered worldly.

There is a "course" of this world which we must not traverse (Ephesians 2:2). John referred to this when he said, "Love not the world" (I John 2:15). He spoke of the system which the world used and the course it followed.

Sometimes one might say, "Well, everybody is doing it." Any time "everybody" is doing something, we should be wary of it. There is a way which seems right to men, but it is a way of destruction (Proverbs 14:12). When Jesus said that there was a "broad way" which leads to destruction, He was talking about those things which "everybody" was doing (Matthew 7:13).

Worldly sports, carnivals, and rock music are a few things which many in worldly circles are participating in, and they are leading the world down its course to destruction. Following that same course will also destroy the victory of the Christian. Anything that is a fad of the day should be seriously evaluated by the Christian lest it pose a danger to his soul.

A present-day fad which has obsessed many is the playing of video games. There is, of course, no apparent harm in a person trying to match wits and skill with an electronic device. People have done the same thing for many years before the electronics age. Then it was usually only a temporary recreation, but now it seems to be an obsession with many. Video rooms are located in every kind of shopping area, and those rooms are usually filled with bored youth plugging away quarters for hours without end.

Newspapers and other news media have spotlighted the alarming effects that idle games are having upon the youth of our day who often have no real goals in life. It now appears that many have adopted the goals to "beat the machine." Such games which are within themselves without any moral wrong can become an obsession and a time-wasting, money-wasting folly.

It is not always easy to determine sins when one is referring to an atmosphere and climate of sin. It is easier to identify some obviously wrong deed. But there is an atmosphere which is not good for the Christian. This is what Paul spoke of as the "course of this world" (Ephesians 2:2). It is the environment in which we moved about freely before coming to Christ. It was a climate in which we felt perfectly at home until God delivered us.

There is a spirit of this age which marks men who are alienated from God. It creates peer pressure among people of the world to participate in worldly activities. Any time the world begins to place pressure on the church by ridicule or by shunning those who live holy, it should be a warning signal. It causes a Christian to feel uncomfortable and out of place when around such worldly individuals.

The course of the world is ever toward greed (Proverbs 1:19; 15:27), lust (Proverbs 6:24-35), sensuality (Galatians 5:17-21), rebellion (II Timothy

3:1-5) and all things which oppose the spiritual nature (Titus 2:12). Once such desires are allowed into the heart, it is hard to arrest them before they cause spiritual death (James 1:14-15).

Moderation in All Things

Paul said for us to let our "moderation be known unto all men" (Philippians 4:5). This should by all means be applied to the selection of amusements. There are many good amusements. God does not wish to take all the fun out of life. He does not withhold anything from us without giving something better in return. As a person draws nearer to God in spiritual things, however, he finds that he needs less and less of this world's amusements to satisfy his needs.

We must be careful of the pleasures we allow ourselves to be involved in. They must first be without sin, and they must not be carried to excess. Every man has leisure time and an inclination for some amusement. A man can be made or marred by the way in which he spends his free time. A certain amount of amusement is beneficial, but multitudes are ruined through worldly entertainment. If a person neglects duty for amusement, he makes a grave mistake regardless of how legitimate the amusement may appear on the surface.

Our pleasures should be pure and unselfish. They are to be enjoyed in a spirit of holiness and consideration for others. God has shown us that He is not opposed to our being entertained by placing within our grasp such an inexhaustible wealth of beauty, grandeur, and challenges of skill. Yet He has made it clear that the Christian must not forsake his purpose and calling in this world.

Moderation is needed in recreation. Moderation is a strength, not a weakness. It requires self-command and self-control. It avoids all extremities of life situations. Moderation does not allow too much or too little of anything. We should not live under too much pleasure or too much labor, too much elation or too much depression, too much affluence or too much poverty.

The Christian will be tempted at times to depart from moderation. He must not forget that every excess has its consequences. Extreme eating is gluttony and causes obesity. Extreme rain causes flood damage, but extreme sunshine brings drought. Extreme physical exercise will break down the muscles that a person is trying to build up. An extreme amount of the Word of God without the Spirit will lead to formalism. Yet an extreme amount of the Spirit without the Word of God causes fanaticism.

Life should not be too much work or too much play, too much sleep or too little sleep.

There are some who feel they do not need to submit to such rigorous principles. They refer to standards which restrain saints from certain amusements as legalism. Yet these same advocates of liberty who have renounced the laws of God and nature have often made themselves servants to laws of their own making (II Peter 2:19). All men need principles by which to guide their lives and keep them moderate in all things.

Karl Menninger said, ''When we are out of harmony there will be illness, chaos, foreboding circumstances, mental strain, improper personal relations. When we are in balance there will be harmony, peace of mind, a buoyant feeling of worthwhileness, and a quiet joy with everything working well. More successes than failures, more completed projects than otherwise, more enjoyable relations with family and friends. When strain, distress, worry, stomachaches and headaches, and personal conflicts are present in your life—analyze, question—Where am I off balance? What am I doing in excess? What am I neglecting?''

Whenever we are guilty of excess in one area of life, it causes neglect in other areas. Sin may come not in the doing of a deed, but in the failure to do what should be done. Entertainment is capable of leading us astray if we do not exercise due moderation. If a person is wasting too much of his leisure time, he may fail to keep the responsibilities that God will call him to account for. In the same way a person who works too many long hours for the good of his personal, physical and mental health is neglecting his rest, fresh air and exercise; and he will reap what he sows.

People who live an unbalanced life will upset the lives of everyone around them. The hypochondriacs, alcoholics, spendthrifts, misers, complainers, frivolous, greedy, selfish, dishonest, conniving, immoral, power-crazy, playboys, and the lazy people are unbalanced in their lives, and they greatly influence others.

God desires His people to enjoy life and discipline themselves to keep the proper balance. The balanced man is useful to God, society, and himself.

Test Your Knowledge

1. Although not as important as spiritual exercise, _____ exercise is important.

2. It is good for Christians to enjoy times of _____ and recreation.

3. The problem in many activities is not in the activity itself, but rather in the _____ of the event.

4. The _____ one listens to can have a pronounced effect on his spirit and attitude.

5. Every recreational activity should pass the test of providing wholesome _____ or _____.

6. All recreation should be a diversion, not an
_____.

7. Christian amusements must not create a climate in which _____ can be produced.

8. The fact that "everybody is doing it" is not a good basis for justifying our amusements. There is a way that seems _____ to men, but it is actually a way of _____.

9. Christians should not give in to _____
_____ to participate in worldly activities.

10. _____ is the primary key to living a balanced life of spiritual and physical activities.

Apply Your Knowledge

Finish now the list of activities that you began earlier by evaluating each activity in the light of the Word of God and basic principles. Be fair and honest with yourself and with God.

There may be some activities you would be better off without. If you think that may be a possibility, why not try your life without them and see what happens? The results can be very positive in your Christian walk!

On the other hand, you may decide that you need more fellowship and activities in your life. You must realize that recreation is important in moderation and proper activities.

Expand Your Knowledge

If you decided you need more Christian interaction and fellowship in your life, you may wonder, "What can I do?" Many wholesome ideas have been included in the next chapter. Though this list is certainly not meant to be exhaustive, you may get some great ideas there.

First, however, read the Scriptures for the chapter as a foundation.

Christian Activities

And the very God of peace sanctify you wholly; and I pray God your whole spirit and soul and body be preserved blameless unto the coming of our Lord Jesus Christ.

I Thessalonians 5:23

Start With the Scriptures

Proverbs 17:22   Colossians 3:23
I Corinthians 9:25   I Timothy 4:8
Philippians 4:8   II Timothy 2:5

The pressures of living are a strain for even the Christian family. Family discipline, budgets, the children's education, and the spiritual needs of the family are all responsibilities of the modern Christian parent. All of these are important and each vies for a prominent place in the Christian home.

Raising a family in the fear of God is a tremendous responsibility. It is physically and emotionally exhausting, and Christians need times of relaxation and recreation to recoup and refresh their strength and energy.

With a keen perception of human frailty, Jesus once said to His tired disciples, "Come ye yourselves apart. . .and rest a while" (Mark 6:31). He knew well the human need for rest and relaxation. As Vance Havner has well said, "If you don't come apart, you'll come apart."

God has the best interests of His creation at heart. He greatly desires for His children to live the highest quality life possible in this world.

Abundant Life

When the Lord comes into a person's life, He brings abundant life. There is a fulness of joy and everlasting pleasure that accompanies God's Spirit (Psalm 16:11). The supply of joy and pleasure is inexhaustible.

God gives a quality of joy and pleasure to life that will never fade. Instead of growing stale, these elements actually increase in the Christian's life as he lives for God. This lasting joy is not typical of experiences in the world.

One man testified that he had lived a wild life, living for a thrill from one party to the next. But since giving his life to God, his most fantastic experiences have involved fellowship with other people of God. He discovered that these new God-given experiences of fellowship caused no later regrets as did his former life.

It is rewarding for the Christian to recognize the value of fellowship through wholesome activities. Activities do not always have to be spiritually motivated to be valuable. It is good to satisfy the physical and social needs of a man as well as the spiritual needs.

Prayer, Bible reading, and witnessing are all readily recognized as valuable activities because they minister to the spiritual needs of a man. While this is certainly true, activities which benefit the physical or social needs of a man should not be discounted. The spiritual man is the most important part of the Christian, yet the physical and social elements are very important.

The Christian will be most blessed and useful to God and society if he will maintain a proper balance of these three human elements—physical, social and spiritual. Maintaining physical activities in his life will keep a Christian healthy. If he stays active socially through the fellowship of other Christians, he will not become withdrawn and introverted. Of course, he should never become so occupied with the physical and social that he neglects the spiritual.

Benefits of Christian Activities

There are many benefits of Christian activities that can enhance the lives of believers. Three basic benefits are considered here.

Activities add zest and vitality to life. Some Christians do not really enjoy living for God as they should. Perhaps it is because they lack the joy of the Lord in their lives.

The joy of the Lord is a principle of the Scriptures; it is like an untapped vein of gold waiting to be discovered and enjoyed. Yet joy will bring more wealth into one's life than all the gold in the world.

God desires for His children to have intervals of pleasure and enjoyment. God never labeled all pleasure as sin for He knew that human pleasure was necessary and good as long as it was kept in the proper perspective. Solomon realized this fact when he said, "A merry heart doeth good like a medicine: but a broken spirit drieth the bones" (Proverbs 17:22).

Recreation relieves the tensions of life. The word *recreation* means "renewal—a process of brightening the often dull routines and burdensome responsibilities inevitable to modern life." Recreation is the refreshment of body or mind after work. It is a needful diversion from the pressures of life.

People of today's modern society are overstimulated and underexercised—a dangerous combination. It is a known fact that stress is a major cause of heart disease. Pressures build up even in the lives of Christians, and those pressures must be released.

Recreation is an excellent way of relieving stress. It can provide needful exercise and at the same time bring essential relaxation to one's body, mind, and soul.

Activities unite the church. It is good for Christian youth and children to see their parents in a fellowship setting other than a church service. This kind of exposure builds relationships with them. They get to see practical Christian living in action.

Adults also need to relate with their peers on a social level. This strengthens bonds between Christians and reinforces them against the enemy.

Fellowship through various Christian activities brings a close bond of unity and comradeship that is beneficial to the church. When they have become close through fellowship, Christians also find it natural to share strength and remain close through trials.

Activities for Fellowship

There are many types of activities from which wholesome Christian fellowship may be derived. The actual benefits that can be obtained through Christian activities are as unique and varied as the activities themselves.

Physical activities. Some forms of recreation provide excellent opportunities for physical exertion. The exercise value alone is quite beneficial for many

Christians. Many occupations today require very little physical effort. Since some exercise is necessary for good health, the Christian may find that he can benefit from the physical aspect as well as enjoy valuable fellowship.

There are some activities for the very active such as basketball or baseball. These along with other various games can generate plenty of activity and fellowship.

An effort should be made to involve even the physically inactive. They should not feel out of place simply because they are not proficient athletes. These individuals can usually become involved in volleyball, softball, or other subdued activities. Horseshoes or Ping-Pong are excellent activities for some who may not feel comfortable with the more physically active games.

It is essential that in any activity there should not be an improper mixing of believers with unbelievers. This does not mean that Christians are to avoid any social contact with sinners, for Jesus gave us an example of being with sinners in an effort to save them. Christians cannot, however, maintain fellowship in a worldly atmosphere.

Excursion activities. There are numerous activities that involve making educational trips or other trips for enjoyment.

Such trips as visiting the zoo, historical sites, or museums and art galleries can provide good fellowship for groups of most any size. These kinds of activities are of good educational value as well as prime opportunities for fellowship.

In some areas special river or ocean cruises provide an excellent Christian activity. Cruise boats can often be rented for short trips of only a few hours' duration. Sometimes a special informative or educational tour is included with the cruise.

Christian men often enjoy fishing. Special arrangements can be made for a day at the lake. In some locations arrangements can be made to charter a deep sea fishing vessel. Such group excursions can often bring unity to the men of a local church. The fellowship alone is very healthy and rewarding to those involved.

Many church outings and picnics can be organized to provide fellowship. When such a gathering is near a river or lake, those who wish may go camping or boating. Of course, different activities will appeal to different individuals. That is why a good variety of activities should be offered.

Social activities. Some activities may be considered social in scope and still provide Christian fellowship.

Christian socials are a good means of providing fellowship and enjoyment for groups of most any size and age. Many of the previously mentioned activities can be enjoyed as well as many wholesome games of spelling, matching wits, and other skills.

Educational and inspirational films can be used in some social activities. Many such films are available through the local public library. Discretion should always be exercised when selecting films. Proper standards of Christian conduct should be the guiding factor of selection.

Another activity that has been successful for some groups is the "lock-in." This is an active night of recreation for young people. Usually conducted in a gymnasium, activities are carefully planned for the entire night. Table games, basketball, volleyball, Ping-Pong, and many other games can be enjoyed by all.

Such "lock-ins" should be properly supervised and monitored. Those participating should stay inside and are permitted to leave only with permission for emergencies. When properly organized, they can be great fun and offer important fellowship to those in attendance.

Dining out is an activity that is always in season and will fit almost any size group. It can provide plenty of enjoyment and fellowship for couples or for a group of Christians. Whether young people or adults, most Christians enjoy this form of entertainment.

An organized form of this activity is the banquet. This is an excellent way for various ministries of the church to enjoy fellowship and also express their appreciation for each other. Banquet programs can entertain and also provide spiritual guidance.

Activities for Personal Enrichment

There are many Christian activities that can provide a sense of personal accomplishment and relaxation.

Reading. Reading various books and periodicals can be relaxing and yet stimulating. They may provide a means of exercising the imagination or of educating the mind—both are important.

There are numerous religious and self-help books and magazines available for the person who enjoys this activity. Naturally, as with all activities, Christian standards must govern what a Christian reads.

Arts. There are many avenues that a Christian can pursue in exercising his artistic ambitions. These avenues of art provide many persons with relaxing pastimes. Art provides a sense of achievement for some individuals. Artistic skills can also be developed and used for God's work in various capacities.

Hobbies. Most all activities for personal fulfillment could be categorized under this heading. Although too numerous to name, hobbies are great for allowing a person to unwind. It is very important that modern Christians learn how to relax and find release from life's many pressures.

Activities for Spiritual Refreshment

Music programs. Participating in various music programs is practical for every age level. From the children to youth and adults, most everyone enjoys music. Those involved in music are not only blessing themselves, but they are also blessing others.

In addition to organizing two or three choirs, a church may have an orchestra comprised of various instruments. This will provide an activity for some in the church and will also add greatly to the church services.

Evangelistic. The Christian should not take the evangelistic activities of the church for granted. There are many ways to be active in this category.

There are regular and revival church services to participate in. These services are not only good activities, but essential for a Christian.

Bible studies and evangelistic outreach are vital activities for any church. Christians will not only find it edifying to participate in Bible studies, but even more of a blessing to teach them to the sinner. There is a special thrill involved in winning the lost to Jesus Christ.

Teaching Bible studies will cause a Christian to study many Bible subjects for himself. This is good for any Christian. He develops Bible knowledge and skills and learns self-discipline.

Prayer meetings unite a church spiritually. They blend the congregation together in spirit and purpose. Prayer stabilizes church members and prepares them for spiritual victories or battles.

Bible quizzing. Bible quizzing is a great activity for youth and children. It creates a spirit of unity and teamwork. Quizzing builds self-discipline and esteem. Most important, it teaches participants the Word of God.

Bible quizzing offers many outlets to youth in the form of district, regional, invitational, and national quizzing matches. These experiences build sound relationships into the lives of many young people.

Special meetings. Many Christian activities can be built around various special meetings. Family-Life and Youth Retreats are two excellent examples. These offer tremendous times of fellowship and spiritual enrichment and provide opportunities for consecration and self-examination.

A fireside consecration service may be held separate from or in conjunction with special retreats. Such gatherings tend to bless and unite church members.

Effectiveness of Christian Activities

The question might be asked, "Are Christian activities really effective in leading sinners to Christ and in preserving Christians?" In fact, there are innumerable instances of such effectiveness.

When sinners are allowed to be around Christians during times of fun and fellowship, they are generally impressed by the happiness of God's people. The joy is contagious, and the unbeliever finds himself participating and enjoying himself with these "unusual people." Many lost individuals have been won to the Lord through such a circumstance.

Two young men from another country were once befriended by a young Bible college student who invited them to go with him to a student recreational social. Though the young men had long hair and looked very out of place, they were heartily welcomed by the other youth. They enjoyed the fellowship and were very attracted to the young people. They began to come around more and more until they both turned their lives around in repentance and they received the Spirit of God. Fellowship and Christian love pointed them to Christ.

Not only are the two young men now Christians, but one has since won his father to the Lord. Now his father, who lives on the other side of the world, may also reach others with the gospel message of Jesus Christ. It all began with the joy of Christian fellowship.

Fellowship month. An activity that proved to be a refreshing experience for an entire congregation was an annual "Fellowship Month." Each couple or family was encouraged to invite two other families with whom they had not shared time and fellowship into their home or take them to a restaurant for dinner. From this experience, new friendships were formed, fresh appreciation was gained for others, and exuberant testimonies of Christian fellowship were the result.

Upon the proper foundation, families can minister in a spiritual fashion to each other. This provides encouragement, promotes friendliness, and develops mutual appreciation between those involved.

Several congregations are experiencing the blessings of cell ministry or Bible fellowship groups. With the capable leadership of a loving and concerned pastor, this type of Christian activity is both enjoyable and instructional in the ways of the church.

Evaluating Our Activities

The question is often asked by many, "What can I do?" It would be impossible to write a manual of Christian activities and list all the good activities as well as those which should be avoided. Actually, an "activity manual" is not what is needed. Christians need to learn how to evaluate their activities.

Some activities are amoral in nature. They are neither moral nor immoral. In them are no good or bad qualities. Only the implications which are attached to them can identify their ethical significance as being right or wrong.

The bottom line is that when choosing activities,

there are at least two things to consider.

What does the local pastor teach? The pastor is the shepherd who watches for the welfare of the sheep. If a pastor feels something will be detrimental to a local congregation, the congregation should abide by his teaching.

How will this affect my brothers and sisters? This must be considered. It is sometimes better to abstain from things that we do not see any harm in just to preserve the unity of the body.

There are many activities confronting the modern Christian. He must be very careful to consider every aspect of the forms of recreation he chooses. He should be sure that it is something that will edify and not destroy. The welfare of the body of Christ should always be the Christian's foremost concern.

Christian activities should be a blessing and not a burden. With love and God's Spirit to guide them, Christians can know which activities to enjoy and which to avoid.

Test Your Knowledge

True or False

_____1. Raising a family in the fear of God is a tremendous responsibility.

_____2. Christ promised believers that He came to bring abundant life.

_____3. Fellowship has no real value in the life of a Christian.

_____4. There are only two elements of mankind which need attention—the physical and social needs.

_____5. One of the many benefits of Christian activities is that they add zest and vitality to life.

_____6. It is not good for children to see adults involved in recreation.

_____7. Reading is a good example of an activity for personal enrichment.

_____8. There are many spiritual activities as well as physical ones.

_____9. Christian activities have had little effect as an evangelistic tool.

_____10. The two main things to consider when evaluating your activities are what the pastor teaches and how it will affect your brothers and sisters in Christ.

Apply Your Knowledge

List three activities, physical or spiritual, that you feel would most benefit your life that you are not presently doing or doing often enough. Set some goals and priorities in your life and challenge yourself afresh.

It is good to evaluate our goals, priorities, and activities occasionally. A life that has no challenge will soon experience boredom. Set some new goals! Interject some new activities into your life! Make some fresh commitments! You may be amazed how much you will benefit from this simple challenge.

Expand Your Knowledge

In addition to reading the Scriptures for the next chapter, try to think of two people who said something especially nice to you in recent weeks. Remember how good you felt? Write down those names and remember them in a special way in your prayers this week.

If you simply cannot think of someone who spoke kindly to you recently, perhaps you can recall two people who were not so nice. Remember how you felt when they spoke harshly to you? Write down their names and pray especially for them this week. Pray that God will strengthen them and help them. Pray that God will bless them!

This simple exercise will help prepare you for chapter ten.

Sound Speech

Sound speech, that cannot be condemned; that he that is of the contrary part may be ashamed, having no evil thing to say of you.

Titus 2:8

A word fitly spoken is like apples of gold in pictures of silver.

Proverbs 25:11

Start With the Scriptures

Psalm 39:1
Proverbs 15:4; 21:23
Matthew 5:34
Ephesians 4:15-31; 5:4

Colossians 4:6
James 1:19-26; 3:1-8; 4:11
II Peter 2:10
Revelation 21:8

Perhaps the most forceful member of the human body is the tongue. The tongue gives emphasis and power to words—words that have the power to sway human emotions.

When someone speaks the words, "I love you," the emotions of the recipient are quickened and his heart is made glad. A defendant feels relief when the jury foreman says, "Not guilty." When the doctor says, "We found no cancer," or the supervisor says, "I am giving you a raise," joy and gladness are brought to that person's heart.

Words also have the power to sadden. When the doctor says, "I am sorry, but it is cancer," grief and fear result. When a telephone call brings news that a loved one is dead, one's heart is made sad. The words, "You're fired," strike anxiety, fear, and sadness in the heart of a suddenly unemployed individual. These are only a few words that can strike a negative influence on the emotions of men. Indeed, the tongue is a powerful member of the body.

The tongue can scratch like a needle, stab like a bayonet, sting like a bee, or kill like a bullet. On the other hand, Christians can employ the tongue in sound speech, as positive influence upon the world. One of the Christian's greatest potential strengths is his or her ability to encourage others.

If the tongue is controlled and used for good, it can communicate joy and express sympathy. Christians can encourage and strengthen each other with words of encouragement. Together they can offer praise to God with their tongues which become instruments of worship.

Taming of the Tongue

God made many wild beasts of the field, yet they can be tamed. The tiger that strikes terror when it is on the loose can be led by a little boy with a single string when tamed and trained. A wolf can be tamed until it exhibits no difference from a domesticated dog. A roaring lion can be the scourge of a village, but he can also be trained to jump through a fiery hoop. Even some serpents have been tamed.

But the tongue cannot be tamed by man. Only God can enable us to control our speech for proper communication.

Although the members of the body can be unruly, many examples could be cited to reveal that men can discipline the various body members to do well. The ear can be trained to listen only to that which edifies. The foot can be trained to walk the path of righteousness, and the hand can be disciplined to work with all might for the Lord, but only God can tame the tongue.

Disciplined Speech

The tongue needs to be controlled perhaps more than any member of the body. The Apostle James said that the tongue is an unruly evil that is full of deadly poison (James 3:8).

The Bible teaches that we should study to be quiet (I Thessalonians 4:11). If a soft answer will turn away wrath, what effect will no answer have on one's enemies? When Jesus was reviled, He answered not a word.

Abraham Lincoln once said it was better to remain silent and be thought a fool than to speak out and remove all doubt. There are times that silence would be the best answer.

"My talent is to speak my mind," said a woman to John Wesley. Wesley answered, "I am sure, Sister, that God wouldn't object if you buried that talent."

Christians who know how to discipline their words are of great blessing and value to the church. Their ability to hold their peace when necessary, yet say the appropriate words when the occasion requires it is very edifying. They are usually highly esteemed and have many friends. Solomon once wrote that "a word fitly spoken is like apples of gold in pictures of silver" (Proverbs 25:11).

Sins of Unsound Speech

There are many sins that evolve from undisciplined speech. One of the most obvious is lying. Hypocrisy and profanity are other verbal sins which are strongly condemned by the Scriptures.

One of the more subtle verbal sins is that of couples sharing intimate details and idle talk of their personal marital relationships. The so-called sexual revolution and an increasingly relaxed attitude toward sexual matters has laid a serious trap for some couples. Matters pertaining to personal intimacies between two married people are sacred and belong only to that couple. Loose and idle talk in this area can break down moral integrity and privacy, and can lead well-meaning couples into adulterous situations.

Although many more verbal sins could be mentioned, we will examine three basic categories of unsound speech.

Flattery. There are few things more offensive to one's dignity than a chameleon-tongued flatterer.

The chameleon is a nimble little lizard which has the ability to change its color to blend with its surroundings. This is similar to the way the flatterer adjusts his philosophies and speech to match those around him. He is as changeable as a chameleon. He humors others in their folly and praises their virtues, but when he meets with someone of another nature, he suddenly changes his color and takes an opposite point of view in his speech.

A flatterer often gives undue and undeserved praise with an impure motive in mind. It may be to secure a favor, to be elevated in regard, or to receive a compliment in return.

A venerable white-haired clergyman filled in one Sunday in the pulpit of a friend. He had hardly arrived home from the church when the doorbell rang and a charming girl of eighteen asked to see him. They talked about the sermon until finally she said, "Oh, won't you please give me a lock of your hair?"

"Certainly, my child," said the old gentleman, flattered at the request. "I'll send it to you tomorrow." And he did.

The following day he had five more requests of the same nature, and he proudly boasted to his wife that he was glad to see he had not yet lost his ability to charm and to please.

All went well until it came to light that the ladies were obtaining locks of his hair for making *hair flowers*. It seems that the white color of the gentleman's hair was just the color that they needed for some of the flowers. It was a very difficult color to find.

The clergyman undoubtedly learned a valuable lesson about flattery and egotism through that experience. Christians should never allow flattery to cause them to think more highly of themselves than they should.

Gossip. Another dangerous sin of unsound speech, and probably the most common, is gossip.

Gossip is idle talk or chatter about the affairs of others. Although the term *gossip* itself does not appear in the Bible, the principle is forcibly illustrated.

Nehemiah set out to repair the walls of the city of Jerusalem. While he was hard at work, Tobiah, Sanballat, and Geshem tried four times through different means to persuade him to quit. Nehemiah responded, "I am doing a great work, so that I cannot come down" (Nehemiah 6:3). After failing four times to discourage Nehemiah, they tried using gossip to accomplish their goal.

Sanballat picked up some idle gossip to use against Nehemiah and all the Jews. But Nehemiah saw through the scheme and said, "There are no such things done as thou sayest, but thou feignest them out of thine own heart" (Nehemiah 6:8).

Many great men of faith in the Bible had to endure the evils of gossip. Gossip caused Daniel to be put into the lions' den. Absalom employed flattery and gossip to influence men against the reign of his father, King David. It caused David many problems and eventually cost Absalom his life.

The Apostle Paul, knowing the danger of gossip, rebuked gossipers as busybodies who idly wander from house to house as *tattlers* (II Thessalonians 3:11; I Timothy 5:13).

The Apostle Peter warned about the danger of intervening in other men's business (I Peter 4:15).

Men often pattern their lives to follow positive, practical rules of conduct. This adds a certain positive strength to one's life as he learns to discipline himself in conduct.

There are also certain negative patterns that a Christian should avoid. There are at least twelve phrases that sometimes suggest gossip, and it would be wise to avoid them. They are:

- *I heard. . . .*
- *They say. . . .*
- *Everybody says. . . .*
- *Have you heard. . . ?*
- *Did you hear. . . ?*
- *Isn't it just awful. . . ?*
- *People say. . . .*
- *Did you ever. . . ?*
- *Somebody said. . . .*
- *Would you think. . . ?*
- *Don't say I told you, but. . . .*
- *Oh, I think it's perfectly terrible that. . . .*

These are only a few of the phrases that often precede gossip-laden conversations. Even if the information is true, it is seldom edifying or needful to discuss it.

There are also seven *mischievous misses* that are often responsible for gossip and idle chatter. They are:

- *Misinformation*
- *Misquotation*
- *Misrepresentation*
- *Misinterpretation*
- *Misconstruction*
- *Misconception*
- *Misunderstanding*

Christians should be very cautious not to fall victim to any of these traps of gossip. The Christian should carefully guard his speech because words cannot be recalled. Words stubbornly reach their object and either edify or destroy.

An author by the name of Theodore Reinking faced execution in 1646 because he had offended King Christian IV of Denmark with a book he wrote. King Christian offered him the alternative of "eating his book" or being executed. Reinking tore the book into shreds, soaked it in soup, and began eating until he had devoured the whole book.

Unfortunately, once words are spoken they become part of the eternal record. People will either be responsible for the damage their words create or be credited for the accomplishments of their words. Jesus said that men would give account for every idle word they speak (Matthew 12:36).

People who gossip seldom have any real friends. Others usually feel that the gossiper cannot be trusted. If he idly chatters about the affairs of others, he is viewed as not being trustworthy.

Gossip is a sign that a person's consecration is waning. When a person begins to get spiritually empty, his speech often deteriorates. There are too many exciting and positive things for Christians to talk about for them to get caught in the negative gossip trap.

Before a person says a word, he should ask himself three very important questions.

- *Is it kind?*
- *Is it true?*
- *Is it necessary?*

Slander. The psalmist David once resolved to control his tongue (Psalm 39:1). What caused David to make such resolution? He had undoubtedly learned the value of sound speech. It is wise to watch carefully the words that one speaks. A Christian never knows when his idle words may return to haunt him. The only solution is self-control before one's words are spoken.

Slander differs from gossip in its intention. When a person gossips, it is not with the express purpose of doing harm. It may cause harm, but a gossiper tells something just for the thrill of telling it. He does not generally intend to harm others through his gossip. A slanderer, however, is different. Slander is told with the express purpose of causing another's character irreparable harm.

The devil is the original slanderer. His name even means *accuser.* His first dealings with man in the Garden of Eden were based on slander. He said, "God doth know that in the day ye eat thereof, then your eyes shall be opened, and ye shall be as gods, knowing good and evil" (Genesis 3:5). The devil was insinuating that God was envious of His creation. He also implied that God was a liar since God had said they would die if they ate the forbidden fruit.

In the testing of Job, Satan slandered both God and Job. He slandered God by suggesting He was a liar, and he slandered Job by implying that he had no spiritual depth. (See Job 1:8-11.)

The devil desires to make evil appear good and good appear evil. This, in fact, is the essence of slander. Slander attempts to cast a bad light upon that which is good; it is inspired by the devil.

The devil hates that which God loves. He hates man because God loves man. Man was created in the image of God, and for this reason God considers the slander of mankind as slander of Himself. When a person strikes out at another human being, whether in words or actions, he is striking out at God. (See Matthew 25:34-46.)

Slander is a terrible sin because it affects the reputation of a man. Slander can tarnish that which man considers so very precious—his name. Solomon wrote that "a good name is rather to be chosen than great riches, and loving favour rather than silver and gold" (Proverbs 22:1). A reputation is similar to a mirror—a blow can break it and one's breath can blur it.

Slander is a grave crime against the honor and dignity of someone. It has been said that a good name is the immediate jewel of the soul. Material things can be replaced when stolen, but a good name is priceless. When a Christian's reputation is stolen by slander, he is left poor indeed.

Someone once said that it is easy to make a mountain out of a molehill—just add a little more dirt. A slanderer just keeps adding dirt. He does not care if the facts are true or false as long as they add fuel to his fire of slander. The slanderer cares only about ruining a reputation.

Slander has been unacceptable in every known civilization.

- Menu—a great legislator of the Hindus said, "The most severe judgment is reserved for the slanderer."
- Solon—prescribed heavy fines for slander.
- Caesar Augustus—prescribed the death penalty for slander.
- Egyptians—When a person was falsely accused, but then proven to have been the victim of slander, the penalty that would have been that of the accused became the penalty of the accuser.

If pagan civilizations condemned slander, how must God feel about it? It is mentioned as one of the seven things that God hates (Proverbs 6:19). If God hates it, then Christians should hate it also.

Slander is a poison as deadly as a scorpion's. The difference is that a scorpion carries its poison in its tail, and a slanderer projects his poison with his speech.

Christians should exercise extreme caution in their conversations. If one's words will not edify the body of Christ, they are better left unspoken. The entire design of the church is for the edification of Christ and His many members.

The intelligent use of sound speech elevates humans above animals. Only mankind can use his speech to bless another and worship God. Satan should never be allowed to use one's speech to hurt a brother or sister or to insult God.

Only through the use of a human tongue can the devil spread his venom of slander. If Christians will simply refuse Satan the use of their tongues, his channel of effectiveness will be cut off.

Through the sound speech of Christians the world can become a better place in which to live. As God's children yield themselves to Him, including their speech, the attacks of Satan against humanity are thwarted. He becomes a helpless dwarf when we take away his weapons—ourselves.

The rule of love is the key. As Christians love each other, they become a mighty force of united strength. Helping and edifying one another through sound speech, the church will march victoriously through the battles of life and each member will receive his eternal reward in glory.

Test Your Knowledge

1. Perhaps the most forceful member of the body is the _____.

2. Christians can discipline their _____ and have a positive influence on the world.

3. Only _____ can tame the tongue.

4. James said the tongue is full of _____ _____.

5. Solomon once said that a word fitly spoken is like _____ __ _____ in _____ __ _____.

6. Three of the basic sins of unsound speech are
_____, _____, and _____.

7. _____ is idle talk or chatter about the affairs of others.

8. Three of the seven *mischievous misses* are
_____, _____, and _____.

9. Words can either _____ or
_____.

10. The rule of _____ is the key to sound speech that edifies others.

Apply Your Knowledge

Try making a special effort to say some nice things to several people in the next few days. Compliment your supervisor or secretary. Let your companion know how much you love them or tell your mother how much she means to you.

See if you can make a list of at least five people you know that you would like to edify through a few kind words. Also, purpose in your heart to say something nice to at least five people that you do not know. See if you can make your grocer's day, or your dentist's, or your mailman's, etc. When you make others feel good, you cannot help but feel good also.

Expand Your Knowledge

Read *Start With the Scriptures* for chapter eleven and consider them carefully. If you are married write down the three characteristics you like best about your companion. If you are dating, write down what you like best about the one you are courting. If you are not married or dating, write down what you would consider to be the most important traits to look for in a companion.

Courtship—
Love—Marriage

Flee also youthful lusts: but follow righteousness, faith, charity, peace, with them that call on the Lord out of a pure heart.

II Timothy 2:22

Start With the Scriptures

Genesis 2:21-24; 39:7-12   Ephesians 5:22-33
Proverbs 18:22; 31:10-31   I Timothy 4:12; 5:1-2, 22
Ecclesiastes 9:9   I Peter 3:1-7
I Corinthians 6:9-20; 7:1-40

Courtship and Love

Next to the choice of Jesus as his Redeemer, the selection of a companion can be the most important decision in a person's life. Since a teenager will probably make this decision within the next ten years of his life, the subject of courtship and marriage is vitally important.

Adolescence. At about the age of twelve, boys and girls pass into a period in which the rapid and dramatic changes occur that bridge the gap between childhood and adulthood. Girls usually begin this development earlier than boys, sometimes as early as age ten. They grow taller and heavier. It is not unusual for girls to act and appear older than boys of the same age at this particular period.

Between the ages of twelve and fifteen, boys often take a sudden growth which usually makes them taller than girls of corresponding age. During these teen years, fellows begin to sprout hair on their upper lips and proudly announce that they have begun to shave.

During this adolescent period, both boys and girls experience important developments in the glandular systems of their bodies. Several of these developments are in preparation for marriage and parenthood.

At this point the dating phase of courtship begins, and it becomes very important for young people to understand Christian principles that govern the conduct between themselves and those of the opposite sex.

Understanding Sex

There are two scriptural reasons for which God created the two sexes: a husband and his wife will enjoy each other's fellowship and together they will have children. (See Genesis 2:21-24.)

Fellowship. God created the first man for the purpose of fellowshiping with him, but He realized that Adam could not be happy without human companionship. For this reason Eve was created as the first female of the human race. From the time of that first union, men and women have found it natural to seek out the companionship of one another.

When boys and girls reach adolescence, they normally experience an instinctive impulse to enjoy the company of members of the opposite sex. This is as normal as getting hungry and thirsty. This attraction will lead to selection for a companion in marriage, in which the fellowship becomes deeper through the years.

Propagation of the race. Courtship is the process in which a boy and girl are attracted to each other, enjoy a period of dating, fall in love, become engaged, and finally are married. This is a natural series of events that most individuals will experience some time in their lives.

It is also very natural for those who enjoy the fellowship of married life to have children. The climax of a loving relationship between a husband and wife is the physical relationship by which children are conceived and brought into the world. This is the plan of God for the human race.

Although marriage and children are part of the normal chain of events that carry out God's plan for the world, it must not be assumed that those who do not marry or have children are abnormal. There are numerous valid reasons one may choose not to marry or have children.

Misuse of Sex

When is sex sinful? Sex becomes sinful when taken out of its proper place, when not safeguarded by common-sense standards, and when not employed for its intended purpose. Sexual relation is always sinful outside of marriage, but within marriage it can be an expression of love and unity—just as God intended. (See I Corinthians 7:1-5.) Adultery and fornication are sins denounced repeatedly in the Bible. (See I Corinthians 6:9; Galatians 5:19; Colossians 3:5; Ephesians 5:3-5.)

One of the curses of modern society is the abnormal emphasis placed upon sex. This abnormal emphasis has taken place in three particular areas.

Entertainment. One reason why the church opposes movies is that commercial entertainment places improper and immoral emphasis upon sex. Divorce, lust, and prostitution are often glorified until viewers develop a warped attitude toward sexual relationships. That which should be pure and wholesome, and reserved for marriage, is often made into a cheap toy for the flesh of carnal mankind. This is often the result of worldly forms of entertainment.

Literature. Newsstands are laden with pornography. This filth has undoubtedly played a great part in promoting sex-related crimes which are occurring at an alarming rate. Many best-selling books feature sordid sexual situations and are unfit for consumption by youth or adults alike.

Advertising. Regardless of whether selling apples or automobiles, advertisers have found it profitable to employ so-called sex appeal. Pictures of scantily clad women adorn many highway billboards and newspaper and magazine advertisements. It is no wonder that youth have become overly sex-conscious when they are constantly confronted with this type of material.

Realizing that these types of pressure and temptation confront the Christian, one must maintain the proper behavior towards members of the opposite sex. Proper conduct is essential if a person is to retain his Christian integrity.

Tips on Dating

The same ideals and standards. While a Christian may be tempted to date an unbeliever, it is not profitable or scriptural to do so. It is never profitable to fellowship those who do not share the same high moral ideals and Christian standards. As a Christian, a young person cannot afford to compromise God-given convictions. Those who date unbelievers may face unnecessary temptations to compromise their Christian ideals.

Some similar interests. It would be very boring for a Christian to go out with someone who was only interested in talking about worldly subjects and going to worldly amusements. These things should hold no interest for the Christian young person. To be with someone who professes to be a Christian, but who is only interested in those things which are unsuitable for Christian behavior, makes for a very boring and uncomfortable evening.

Maintaining Moral Purity

When young people become seriously attached to the companion they will likely marry, they often face new and more dangerous temptations. Probably the most dangerous is the temptation to commit fornication.

Many potentially beautiful relationships are destroyed because couples conduct themselves improperly and kill their love and respect for each other. This can result from being too intimate with each other.

Petting destroys confidence and the respect young people have for each other. This lost respect may not be realized until after marriage, but it will eventually appear.

If a young person will keep himself pure, it will pay big dividends later. There will be increased confidence, respect and happiness. The blessings of God will more likely be upon the marriage. Young people must remember that the curse of God is on sin, and one can never sin and be happy.

Wrong Reasons for Marriage

One must be sure his motives are right for seeking to marry. Some people marry for the wrong reason and pay a high price. Seven of the wrong motives will be considered at this point.

Marriage as an escape mechanism. Some marry in an effort to escape circumstances which they consider worse than being married. Others marry to escape being passed by. They are afraid of being an "old maid" or an "old bachelor."

Some may marry to get even with someone such as their mother or father or someone who has jilted them. These are all wrong reasons for marriage.

Marriage on the basis of beauty. Too many marriages are based on physical attractiveness. This may have its place in the selection of a mate, but it must never be the sole consideration. Physical beauty will not last forever, and it certainly cannot be a sustaining force through life's trials.

Marriage for convenience. A young lady might marry a man because his job sounds exciting or because she would like the security of marriage. These factors should be considered, but they must not be the sole basis for marriage.

Marriage for sexual gratification. Some young people are guided into marriage by lust, and this is usually a sure way into tragedy. Not only is lust a sin; it can never take the place of genuine love and care. Only love can hold a marriage together through the turbulences of life.

Marriage on short notice. A few weeks is not enough time for couples to become sufficiently acquainted. Young people sometimes marry on short notice only to find that had they known each other better they would never have married.

Marriage at too young an age. Teenagers are still growing into maturity, physically and mentally. It is unlikely that they have settled their attitudes, ideals and philosophies of life. For all of these reasons it would be far safer and wiser to delay marriage for a few more years.

Marriage to reform the mate. If there is a trait in a potential mate that is undesirable, the chances are marriage will not change that person. In fact, it may only succeed in bringing out the undesirable traits even more.

The Right Reasons to Marry

Love. The most important reason, although not the only reason, to marry is for love. Love is not all that counts. It is not true that love will always find a way. It is undoubtedly the greatest element of strength in marriage, but there are other factors which should be considered.

Compatibility. Another reason for marriage beyond love is compatibility. Although it is sometimes overlooked, compatibility adds great strength to marriage.

Before two young people marry, they should be positive that their personalities do not clash. Experience teaches us that there are some people we are more naturally drawn to than others. The more we know about them the better we like them. On the other hand, there are other people with whom we clash from the start. It is tragic when a man and woman are united together in the close bonds of marriage when they are incompatible. They will find it very difficult to get along together through the years of marriage.

Congeniality. Some have said that opposites should marry and that people with the same natures should never marry. This is simply not true.

Albert L. Murray in his book, *Youth's Marriage Problems* states: "All attempts to unite people of conflicting types in intimate companionship fail. The materialist and the idealist, the cynic and the conservative, the skeptical and the appreciative, the demanding and the sympathetic, the rigid and the liberal, the sexually active and the passive, the unscrupulous and the puritanical have almost insurmountable obstacles to overcome if they are to achieve unity, and only by constant compromise can they live harmoniously. There can be no satisfying comradeship, sharing of interest and feeling of security in the presence of a person decidedly contrary in temperament and philosophy of life, of one who holds convictions and standards opposed to those of the other."

Similarities. It is good to choose a mate that has a similarity of background. This is certainly not the sole factor to consider; nonetheless, it is an important consideration.

Beyond the similarities of upbringing one might consider similarity of education, similarity of taste, and similarity of interests.

These are all elements that should be considered before marriage. There are also some guidelines that will help a couple have a happy home once they are married.

A Happy Home

The question is, "Do we want a happy home, and are we willing to pay the price of having one?" God's Word explains how to have a happy home. There are numerous keys to having a happy home. We will consider four of them.

Discipline. Both self-discipline and parental discipline of children are needful to maintain a good home environment. The chief value of any discipline is orderliness. If a home is not united, but is disorganized and divided, that home suffers from a lack of discipline.

Parents must first discipline themselves. Some parents might leave things lying around the house or leave chores undone until later, having to do them at the last minute. Some might not control their appetites. Parents should ask themselves, "Do I exercise discipline in my conduct within the home?" If parents are not disciplined themselves, they cannot expect to discipline their children effectively.

The Christian's walk with the Lord also requires discipline. Paul wrote to Timothy, "Study to shew thyself approved unto God" (II Timothy 2:15). The word *study* means to "give diligence" or "be disciplined." The word *disciple* is derived from the word *discipline*. This signifies that it takes diligence and discipline to walk with the Lord. It requires discipline for a Christian to have a time to pray, read the Bible, witness, or be regular in church attendance.

Parental discipline of the children is also important in the home. In a healthy Christian home, children are taught to do right and are punished when they do wrong. The Book of Proverbs has much advice about the proper discipline of a child. Strict discipline is proof of a parent's love. "He that spareth the rod hateth his son: but he that loveth him chasteneth him betimes" (Proverbs 13:24).

Devotion. Also necessary for a happy home is devotion. Devotion to one another within the family as well as devotion to the Lord are both important.

There is an extreme lack of loyalty within many families today. Children fight with brothers and sisters; husbands fight with wives; parents fight with their children. God did not ordain this type of behavior for the family.

A spirit of devotion, love, and loyalty should prevail in Christian homes. The family unit is just that—a unit. If it is to function properly and in unity, there must be a sense of loyalty between every family member.

Why has devotion to one another in many families dissipated? Possibly it is that some families have forgotten how to serve one another. A family, like a church, needs to know the value of giving to others. Both exist for the purpose of serving. Harmony cannot exist in an environment where each person is demanding, asking, and taking—always being ministered unto but never ministering to others. When such conditions exist, the homes involved are not happy.

More important than devotion to each other is devotion to the Lord. God designed the family to be a spiritual body. As is the case with the church, one of the main functions of the family is corporate worship. The family should have times of unified worship and devotion in the home. These times together will strengthen the bonds of unity among the family members as well as with the Lord.

Discussion. Another necessity in order to have a happy home is discussion. Interviewed members of broken homes often point to one cause of failure more than any other—lack of communication. A good question to ask ourselves is, "Do we have open lines of communication in our home?" Do our children feel free to come to us with their problems, no matter how trivial they may seem to us, with confidence that we will listen with understanding and offer good advice? If the answer is yes, there is probably good communication in that home.

In a busy society with an accelerated pace, the home has suffered greatly. Husbands and wives are often too busy to take time for each other. Parents are sometimes too busy to take time for the children. Even the children are too busy at times for one another.

If family members are too busy to talk to one another, they should rearrange their priorities. Perhaps they are involved in too many activities. Parents may be working too many hours. Whatever must be done to insure that we have valuable communication time with our family should be done. Communication will help insure the survival of the home.

Determination. A fourth necessity for a happy

home is determination. Christians can only have a happy home if they are willing to sacrifice for it. We must be determined that our family will be harmonious, united, successful, and happy.

Living in a family is a great privilege. When properly instituted, the home is similar to Heaven. In Heaven Christ will be the center; worship, fellowship, and unity will revolve around Him.

Living in a family is also a great responsibility. It is an opportunity to minister, to sacrifice, to serve, and to grow. But all these things require determination.

We need to ask ourselves if our homes have the four necessities for happiness:

1. Discipline
2. Devotion
3. Discussion
4. Determination

If so, there will be less chance for division in the home. There should be no dissension and no dissolution. There will be, however, new direction and a new dimension of happiness and harmony in the home that follows God's design.

Test Your Knowledge

True or False

_____1. Adolescence is the period of development in which children begin to awaken to the opposite sex.

_____2. Fellowship and the propagation of the race are the two most basic reasons for two sexes.

_____3. Since God communed with Adam, the first man, there was really no need for Adam to have human companionship.

_____4. There are at least two things that persons who date should have in common.

_____5. Christians who date unbelievers are strong and will not face any unusual temptations that other Christians do not face.

_____6. *Petting* while dating destroys confidence and respect that young people have for each other.

_____7. The reason why a person decides to marry is not really important.

_____8. Marriage should never be entered into solely on the basis of physical attraction.

_____9. If a prospective companion has an undesirable trait, he or she will probably change to suit your taste after a few years of marriage.

_____10. Discipline, devotion, discussion, and determination are the four basic ingredients of a happy home.

Apply Your Knowledge

Respect for others and willingness to give in a relationship unselfishly are probably the two most lacking, yet vital factors in serious relationships today. God so loved the world that He gave. If we are not willing to give in a relationship, we do not really love.

Whether you are married or still dating, try being more thoughtful of the one you love more than yourself. Think of some ways in which you can surrender your will to the will of your companion.

The best way to the heart of another is by thinking of him instead of ourself. Thoughtfulness is a guaranteed way of reviving a dying relationship.

Expanding Your Knowledge

Research the background and origin of Halloween, using a good encyclopedia. Make a written report of your discoveries before reading the Scriptures for the next chapter.

You may be very surprised that religious nations observe Halloween when you become aware of its origin and history. The events surrounding Halloween are closely associated with chapter twelve which you are about to read.

The Occult

But the fearful, and unbelieving, and the abominable, and murderers, and whoremongers, and sorcerers, and idolaters, and all liars, shall have their part in the lake which burneth with fire and brimstone: which is the second death.

Revelation 21:8

Start With the Scriptures

Exodus 7:11
Leviticus 19:31
Deuteronomy 18:10-12
I Samuel 28:7-14
Isaiah 8:19

Jeremiah 27:9
Acts 8:9; 13:6-12; 16:16-18;
   19:13-19
Galatians 5:19-21
Revelation 9:20-21; 21:8;
   22:15-16

The occult is based upon several philosophies. First, no single power is recognized as having ultimate control over the universe. This places occultism in the realm of idolatry. It is a flagrant rejection of God's authority and Word. The occult acknowledges a myriad of evil forces which influence mankind.

Secondly, since members of the occult accept no single supreme power, they believe there is a way to contact the forces that do exist and manipulate them to their benefit. This pseudo-science is called the curious arts. It is the process of discovering esoteric and unrevealed knowledge of the universe. It is mysterious, dark, and secretive, and man seems to have a propensity toward the strange and different. He is very curious about that which he does not know. It is that curiosity the devil used to deceive the first couple in the Garden of Eden when he promised, "Ye shall be as gods, knowing good and evil" (Genesis 3:5).

Evidence of men delving into the unknown world of magic goes back to antiquity. Pictures have been found on cave walls depicting animals stuck with darts, usually colored with red paint. These are not just the work of an artist. They stemmed from the superstitious idea that it would bring success in hunting. The spirit in the drawing would supposedly be brought to life by the red paint which signified blood. They believed the spirit would then be transferred to the animal they soon would find and bring them a successful hunt.

The Bible does not deny the power of the occult. Modern culture would like to ignore the reality of any power, outside of God, that could influence life in this world. The Bible acknowledges, however, the presence of various satanically inspired phenomena.

Thirdly, since they believe there is a way to know the secrets of these forces and control them, they feel the exercise of this knowledge can come only as a gift or revelation from that power. For that reason, various methods are employed in efforts to contact these powers. Seances, ouija boards, crystal balls, tarot cards, horoscopes, and vibrations are some of the mediums of contact with the spiritual power which lies beyond man's normal grasp.

Evil Character of the Occult

God only allows man to have a certain amount of

knowledge or revelation about the spirit world and about the future. The future belongs to God, and man was made for His glory. For that reason, God has given man a role within the framework of the drama of redemption.

God reveals Himself to men for the purpose of redemption, but men are often not satisfied with limitations of knowledge. He sometimes would like to discover more knowledge than God is willing for him to know.

Man's curiosity can cause him to desire to be God, knowing good and evil. The devil uses this curiosity to entice man to look to him for enlightenment. The general term for this endeavor is called magic. It is the art of bringing about results beyond man's power through a medium of spirits. These spirit forces are called demons or evil spirits.

Some people fake occultic power through jugglery and sleight of hand. But the devil, a great imitator, uses incantations and other rituals in the same way God communicates with His children through prayer. Satan communicates through drugs, rock music, and other magical formulas in the same way that God interacts with His people through their worship.

In the same way that God requires righteousness and moral integrity before one can fellowship Him, the devil is influenced by immorality and rebellion. The prophet Samuel told Saul that his rebellion was as the sin of witchcraft, and his stubbornness was as iniquity and idolatry (I Samuel 15:23). This was true because rebellion, idolatry and witchcraft all reject God's authority in life and allow one's will to be controlled by a force other than God.

Forms of Occult Practices

There are many occultic practices condemned in the Bible. They range from total possession of a person by demons to the use of charms and horoscopes to find answers for the future or to ward off evil spirits.

Contact with these abominable spirits was made through certain rites. The rites often began with a trance which was brought about by the utterance of certain enchantments.

After contact was made with the evil spirit, there would be a rite of various actions to convey the requests of those making contact. Usually there was an imitation of the desired action such as pins being stuck into the doll as mentioned earlier. The desired action must be conveyed some way to the evil spirit.

The person who brings the action about, usually a witch (female), wizard (male witch), sorcerer, or medicine man, to name a few, must be in harmony with the evil spirit. He must not break any taboo of the order, and he must be in the right emotional state to obtain the requested action.

Spirit contact. The various forms of these occult practices cover a wide range of activity. Divination is one means of contact. Divination is finding secret knowledge which God has considered illegitimate for man to know. It is accomplished by either reading signs or by the use of mediums. It is now usually known as fortune-telling. Divination is sometimes sought through tarot cards or palm reading. When direct contact is attempted with the spirit, it is known as a seance. (See Numbers 22:7; 23:23; Deuteronomy 18:10-14; Joshua 13:22.)

Witchcraft includes all areas which deal with evil spirits in a personal relation such as sorcery, soothsaying, and wizardry. These mediums cause spirits to appear, raise spirits and practice soothsaying. They often use the assistance of a familiar spirit (Exodus 22:18; Deuteronomy 18:10; I Samuel 15:23).

The augur looks for omens. A charmer binds spells on his victim. The necromancer communicates with the dead.

Superstitions. Most superstitions are supposed to ward off evil spirits. Rather than trying to contact the spirit, the superstitious person, or sometimes the charmer and enchanter, tries to avoid the spell of the evil spirit. Superstitions are usually formed by resemblances which suggest a relationship between similar things.

People who hold the superstitious beliefs often have strange customs and theories:

- Usually the right hand and the right side of the body are normal in human activity. The left side reverses this norm and supposedly takes on a magical quality.
- The left hind foot of the rabbit then becomes a charm for good luck.
- If one looks at the new moon for the first time over his left shoulder and simultaneously turns the silver in his pocket (symbol of the moon), it will supposedly reverse the norm (bad luck one has had) and bring good luck.

To a person who does not rely on superstition, but rather trusts God for the providences of life, these things appear foolish. But there are many caught up in such superstitious practices who sincerely believe these things work. There are still some who will drive an axe into the floor near the kitchen table when there has been a tragic accident in the family. This is supposed to ward off the evil influence and keep the person from dying.

Some people believe that spirits live in images. This created the superstition that it is bad luck to break a mirror because one disturbs the spirit in the mirror. The practice of knocking on wood was brought about in a similar fashion. Since some people believed that spirits lived in trees, knocking on wood was supposed to acknowledge the spirit so it would not bother them.

Most other superstitions also carry an idea of influence by spirits. Some still feel odd about walking under a ladder even though they might not think of an evil spirit influence. Yet, the very fact that they are fearful shows a lack of trust in God and a belief that some strange influence is there.

Hotels seldom have a thirteenth floor and Friday the thirteenth is considered unlucky by many. Some feel that bubbles in a teacup or itching skin is an indication that somebody is coming to see them. A blister on the tongue supposedly indicates a lie has been told, and a tingling fear indicates that somebody is talking about the person who has the feeling. Cold shivers on a person is supposed to indicate that someone is walking over his future grave.

Some of these situations may be associated with natural history, but they all indicate an influence by the spirit world.

Many people follow the horoscope religiously, not realizing that it is associated with idolatry and witchcraft. They fail to understand that it is relying upon a power other than God. The horoscope philosophy rejects God's restraints upon man's knowledge of the future and rejects His care and protection as trustworthy.

If any of these superstitions should bother a person, he needs to seek God for deliverance. One should feel no squeamishness when a black cat runs across the trail in front of him. Nothing should hinder a person's going back to the house to get something after he has left. Spilling salt should only make a person feel bad that he has wasted a good thing. Meeting a funeral procession or stepping on a sidewalk crack has no effect upon one's future. A knife can be given every Christmas and it will never cut any friendship. If an umbrella is opened inside, it could damage some furniture, but it will not cause bad luck.

Charms. Part of the condemnation against the wanton women of Jerusalem was their use of crescents, the moon-shaped amulets used for counter charms. They were worn around the neck to protect against evil spirits and were an acknowledgement of idolatry (Isaiah 3:18).

This same thing is done today with a rabbit's foot, horseshoe, or lucky penny. Most people who carry these items may not realize the seriousness of their iniquity, but the Bible clearly indicates that God will condemn men who look to any power other than Him for security.

Hosea mentioned the need for his wife (as a figure of Israel) to put away her "whoredoms out of her sight" (Hosea 2:2). He spoke of the nose ring, which was a charm to counter the curse of the evil eye. There was an idea that some people had an evil eye and could cast a spell, usually a curse, upon a person. She was also commanded to cast her adulteries from "between her breasts." This referred to the necklace, worn as an amulet, to defend the wearer against the evil eye. This same idea of an evil eye, or an evil one who can influence a person, is the source of wearing a cross around the neck or putting a statue in the car to protect one while traveling.

Paul made reference to the idea of the evil eye when he asked the Galatians, "Who hath bewitched you?" (Galatians 3:1). He was not saying that such an evil eye had any real effect, but he used it as an illustration to say, "As people are put under a spell by an evil eye, so you Galatians have been deceived by these Judaizers."

The Bible's Condemnation of the Occult

Because God recognizes the power behind occult practices, He consistently forbids participation in any form of occultism. God drove out the Canaanites before Israel and expressed His displeasure with anyone who followed such abominations as witches and sorcerers (Deuteronomy 18:10-14). God condemned those who would burn their children in the fire. He also named the practices of divination, soothsaying, augurs, sorcery, charmers, mediums, wizards, and necromancers as being especially abominable to Him.

God recognizes all forms of occultism as rivals to His care and protection. God not only condemns the extremity of demon possession but also the use of ouija boards and horoscopes. He demanded that anyone found looking to such devices be put to death (Exodus 22:18; Leviticus 19:26, 31; 20:6, 27; Micah 5:12). God considered these practices deceptive (Isaiah 44:25; 57:3; Jeremiah 27:9; Ezekiel 22:28; Zechariah 10:2; Malachi 3:5).

One of the things which King Josiah did that pleased the Lord was that he put away the mediums, wizards, the teraphim, the idols and all the abominations that were seen in the land of Judah and Jerusalem. He did this that he might establish the words of the Law which were written in the book that Hilkiah the priest had found in the house of the Lord. (See II Kings 23:24.)

God considered calling upon an idol and the invoking of an evil spirit basically the same. Those who called on evil spirits basically followed six steps:

- They would call upon the spirit by saying something like, "I call upon you; I summon you; come to me; help me."
- The name of the spirit was then called.
- A description of the spirit was given.
- The benevolent things which the person felt the spirit was capable of bequeathing were mentioned.
- Recollection was then made about any past performance of the spirit.

- The request was made.

When these steps were followed using certain amulets, potions, secret writings and sacrifices, the person made contact with the spirit. Hence seances and idol worship are the same. Both are calling on something other than God for the very things God wants man to call upon Him for. It is obvious why God becomes angry when every step a man takes in turning to idolatry and witchcraft takes that man away from God.

In the Early Church converts burned their books of curious arts (Acts 19:19). Any item possessed by Christians today which speaks of witchcraft should be burned. This includes books, horoscopes, records, fetishes, tarot cards, emblems of evil spirits, and ouija boards.

Anything which is associated with drugs should also be discarded. The New Testament directly connects drug traffic with evil spirits and the occult. The magician was a mixer of potions and is what we now call a drug pusher. (See Revelation 21:8; 22:15.) The New Testament calls these dealings sorcery (drugs) and magic (Galatians 5:20; Revelation 9:21; 18:23).

The potions of their day were made of poisons from herbs to bring about spells. They were little different from the various forms of drugs today with their poisons, such as marijuana and all other supposedly mind-expanding drugs.

No man can serve two masters (Matthew 6:24). God will not accept the man who worships at the temple of idols and at the same time tries to worship at God's altar (I Corinthians 10:21). Idolatry is a deadly thing. We must not provoke God to jealousy. Jealousy is the fear of being displaced, and when God sees anyone allow another to take His place, He becomes a jealous God.

God does not want us to experiment with anything associated with occultism. Nor does He want us to study about it beyond a general knowledge. This type of study is adequate for our understanding, without going into great depths of esoteric knowledge. Paul told the Romans it was better to be wise about the good and simple concerning the evil (Romans 16:19).

To make in-depth studies in such subjects as demonology may call them to close and careful attention and cause trouble. We may study how to conquer our enemy and learn his devices, but we must not become involved in the intricacies of his worship. There is no reason to lay our souls open to the enticements of demons and our bodies to their obsessions.

There is a real demonic power behind witchcraft and other forms of occultism. God recognized this when He condemned all use of spiritual forces outside of Himself (Deuteronomy 18:10-12). He did not deny that the Egyptians really turned their rods into serpents and performed other supernatural feats during the time of the plagues (Exodus 7 through 11). It was clearly not jugglery or sleight of hand. God recognized the Python spirit in the girl who followed Paul (Acts 16:16). In casting out demons He recognized their power (Mark 1:24; Luke 4:34; Matthew 8:29).

The fact that the apostles continued to deal with occult situations as recorded in the Book of Acts further proves the continued work of evil. Simon Magus wanted to add Holy Ghost power to his sorceries (Acts 8:19-24). Bar Jesus, or Elymas, resisted Paul and Barnabas (Acts 13:4-12). Nowhere does the Bible even hint that this power was a fraud. It was real and was dealt with as a reality.

Not only does God recognize it as a reality, but He calls it an abomination, punishable by death. The occult is serious with God because it is idolatry. Thus, He does not want us to be curious about these things. A person can too easily be trapped by his curiosity. The progression to oppression, depression, and finally possession may be imperceptible, but it is sure. It is like quicksand—unseen and treacherous. A person may be past recovery before he knows that he is even in danger.

We must stay on guard and maintain a strong, spiritual walk with God. There are three basic areas to guard:

Christians should avoid every form of evil spirits. They should stay away from horoscopes, ouija boards, palm readers, fortune-tellers and anything that may have a link to satanic influence.

Christians must avoid the secondary or indirect avenues to the evil spirits, such as rock music, drugs and charms (amulets) that are rituals of Satan.

Christians must maintain the Holy Ghost experience at all times so that He that is within them will be greater than he that is in the world (I John 4:4).

Test Your Knowledge

1. The occult acknowledges a myriad of _____ forces which influence man.

2. The knowledge of the _____ belongs only to God.

3. Satan uses man's curiosity to entice him to seek _____ through magic.

4. Rebellion, idolatry, and witchcraft all deny God's _____.

5. _____ is the process of finding secret knowledge which God has not given to man.

6. _____ includes all areas which deal with evil spirits in a personal relation such as sorcery, soothsaying, and wizardry.

7. The Bible condemned some women of Jerusalem who wore _____ to protect themselves against evil spirits.

8. God condemned in the Bible any form of the
_____.

9. Two men who evidenced occultic power in the
Book of Acts were Bar Jesus, or _____
and _____ _____.

10. God considers the occult as an _____,
and it is punishable by death.

Apply Your Knowledge

WARNING: The Bible has determined that curiosity in the realm of the occult can be hazardous to your spiritual health.

It is essential that Christians do not idly and curiously toy with or experiment with the occult. Even an in-depth study of the occult is not good or edifying for a child of God. Here are three practical rules to follow:

1. *Avoid contact with the occult or devices of the occult.* There is no reason for a Christian to experiment with such evil forces. It is only inviting trouble.

2. *Recognize Satan's power.* Do not deny his power for it is second only to that of Almighty God. This is not to honor or glorify him, but only to realize that he does influence men in a powerful way toward evil.

3. *Realize you are a child of God.* Do not fear Satan because He who is in you is greater than all the forces of hell. The church has been given power and dominion over every evil spirit.

Expand Your Knowledge

Read the Scriptures in preparation for chapter thirteen. The publication *Victorious Living for New Christians* would be an excellent addition to this final chapter. It may be obtained from Word Aflame Press, 8855 Dunn Road, Hazelwood, Missouri 63042.

Perfecting Holiness

Having therefore these promises, dearly beloved, let us cleanse ourselves from all filthiness of the flesh and spirit, perfecting holiness in the fear of God.
II Corinthians 7:1

Start With the Scriptures

Psalm 29:2	Colossians 2:10; 3:1-6
Romans 6:19	I Thessalonians 4:7
II Corinthians 3:18; 4:10-11	Hebrews 12:1, 2, 14
Galatians 4:19	I Peter 1:16
Ephesians 2:10; 4:12-15	II Peter 1:1-8
Philippians 1:5-6	Revelation 19:7-8

In concluding our study of Christian standards, we must emphasize that the final responsibility for living a victorious, overcoming life rests with the individual himself. God is not interested in having a church full of puppets. He created people to have the power of choice. He desires His children to live holy lives separated from the world, but He also desires that His people make that choice of their own volition.

Each individual has to decide whether or not he

will live a dedicated life for Jesus Christ. The decision is whether to live for God or to live for the world. Defeat comes by loving the world, but victory becomes a reality when we truly love Jesus. Where is our heart—in the world or in the church? The answer to this question determines our entire Christian walk.

The Bible clearly places the responsibility of choice on every person. We alone decide where to place our love. God has required that we "love not the world, neither the things that are in the world" (I John 2:15).

A special blessing is promised to those who have set their affections upon Jesus. "Because he hath set his love upon me, therefore will I deliver him" (Psalm 91:14).

If a person loves some worldly habit more than he loves Jesus, he will never be willing to give it up. On the other hand, if he loves Jesus, there will be a conviction of sin followed by genuine repentance. True repentance will break every unclean habit. If a man has difficulty giving up the cigarette habit, it is because he does not want to. He evidently loves to smoke more than he loves the Lord. The battle is won or lost in his heart.

A man was bound by the habit of gambling. Each Saturday evening he would gamble away his weekly paycheck. At home his wife and children were hungry. He would pray and cry with bitter tears, but still repeat his folly the following Saturday night. What was his trouble? He loved to gamble more than he loved his family and more than he loved Jesus Christ. His prayers and tears did not make his repentance genuine.

In the study of Christian standards it should be emphasized that we can live holy lives. The will of God is always possible. God will never require of us that which we cannot do. There is never any reason to compromise with the world. A Christian can maintain high standards of holiness and live a victorious, overcoming life.

Godly Aspirations

An important priority in living successfully for God is to set proper goals. One must know what he desires from God and then reach toward that spiritual attainment with singleness of mind and heart. A drifter never reaches great spiritual heights. He is often washed back and forth upon the worldly shoals of carnal temptation. He goes up and down with the tide of moods and emotions. However, the Christian who sets the goal of reaching spiritual perfection in Christ will grow and mature in every phase of Christian living.

One young man once set his goal to be a millionaire before he was forty years old. This was his chief ambition in life and all his ability and energy were directed toward that end.

He achieved his desired goal many times over. Not only was he a millionaire by forty, but he was a multi-millionaire. It would have been much better if he had set some spiritual goals for his life as well. In the same way that young man was able to reach a material goal, each Christian has the opportunity to gain eternal wealth if he sets spiritual goals.

The psalmist David wrote concerning his desired goal in life: "One thing have I desired of the LORD, that will I seek after; that I may dwell in the house of the LORD all the days of my life, to behold the beauty of the LORD, and to inquire in his temple" (Psalm 27:4).

We may also read of the singleness of desire possessed by the Apostle Paul: ". . .but this one thing I do, forgetting those things which are behind, and reaching forth unto those things which are before, I press toward the mark for the prize of the high calling of God in Christ Jesus" (Philippians 3:13-14).

The starting point in experiencing a victorious, overcoming Christian life is the setting of spiritual goals. The Christian should set his heart upon being his very best for the Lord. He should never be satisfied with a mediocre experience, but rather desire to excel in all things relating to his relationship with Jesus.

Perfecting Holiness

"Having therefore these promises, dearly beloved, let us cleanse ourselves from all filthiness of the flesh and spirit, perfecting holiness in the fear of God" (II Corinthians 7:1).

There are two truths taught in this Scripture that we should carefully consider:

- Holiness must be perfected. We never reach the ultimate in spiritual attainment. There is always growth and maturing that must take place as we learn to turn our backs upon sin, die out to carnal desires, and dedicate ourselves to lives of obedience in the will of God.
- The responsibility for perfection lies within the individual Christian. He himself is responsible for whether he is a carnal, careless believer, or a spiritual, dedicated child of God. He is the one who must perfect holiness in his own life.

There are other Scriptures which teach the Christian's responsibility for his own spiritual growth. "But grow in grace, and in the knowledge of our Lord and Saviour Jesus Christ" (II Peter 3:18). "Work out your own salvation with fear and trembling" (Philippians 2:12). The question is how can the Christian accomplish this? In reply to this question let us examine four verses of Scripture which will help us know what to do:

- *"Let us cleanse ourselves from all filthiness of*

the flesh and spirit. . ." (II Corinthians 7:1). Through repentance the Christian separates himself from everything that is filthy. He refuses to have a part in any perverted act or unclean thought. Not only must the Christian lay aside all unclean habits such as tobacco, drugs, pornography and illicit sex, but also everything that would contaminate his attitude such as jealousy and hatred.

• *"Let us lay aside every weight, and the sin which doth so easily beset us. . ." (Hebrews 12:1).* There are many hindrances to dedication. It is our responsibility to lay aside everything which would discourage us from living a holy life.

• *"Denying ungodliness and worldly lusts, we should live soberly, righteously, and godly. . ." (Titus 2:12).* When we deny something, we turn our back upon it. We refuse to entertain it. This the Christian must do with ungodliness and worldly lusts. Before one can live soberly, righteously, and godly, all ungodliness and worldly lusts must be removed from his life.

• *"And he gave. . .pastors and teachers; For the perfecting of the saints. . ." (Ephesians 4:11-12).* For the purpose of perfecting saints, Jesus has placed in His church pastors and teachers. Understanding the purpose of the ministry, the young Christian should faithfully attend all church services and Bible studies. He should be willing to submit himself to his pastor and be taught. Obedience to the teaching of God's Word and the counselling of the man of God will certainly develop spiritual growth.

We Can Live Holy Lives

A young man who frequently sang solos in church had a song which he sang on many occasions. The song was entitled, "If I Can Just Make It In." Finally, the pastor spoke to the young brother, "Please do not sing that song again. We are not interested in just barely making it in. We are looking forward to an abundant entrance.''

That which the pastor said is very true. The child of God has been given an abundant life. The hope of salvation the child of God has must never be questioned. The Christian has been saved! He has been promised a victorious entrance into the kingdom! The Christian can live an overcoming life and make it into heaven!

Victory can be claimed over every enemy. We can defeat the world, the flesh and the devil. If we keep our eyes upon Jesus, He will not let us fail.

We must look to Jesus who is the finisher of our faith. ''Looking unto Jesus the author and finisher of our faith. . .'' (Hebrews 12:2).

Jesus is not only the source and originator of our faith, but also the One who finishes that which He begins. The Apostle Paul emphasized this truth in his letter to the Philippian church: ''Being confident of this very thing, that he which hath begun a good work in you will perform it until the day of Jesus Christ'' (Philippians 1:6).

It is not the Lord's will that one of His children should fail. The cross is not too heavy; the Christian life is not too hard. It is the devil's lie to say that we cannot live for God. There is no temptation too great that we cannot resist. There is no sacrifice so great that we cannot make it. No matter what opposition, persecution, ridicule, and fierce battle the Christian may encounter, a victorious life is more than possible.

The Christian is a new creature in Christ. Old things have passed away and all things are new. The born-again child of God finds that holiness is the natural way of life. It is not difficult to shed the old worldly habits of sin when one is filled with the Holy Spirit.

There is a type of maple tree in eastern Canada

which stubbornly holds onto its leaves in the fall. The cold, north wind cannot blow them off. The snow and hail cannot beat them to the ground. The frost seems unable to freeze the leaves so they will let go. They rattle all winter as the wind blows through the trees. However, in the spring the leaves quietly fall without a struggle. What caused the difference? The new sap flowing up the trunk of the tree into the new buds caused the old leaves to fall.

This is an excellent illustration of the born-again Christian. When one is filled with the Holy Ghost, worldly habits and fashions such as the theater, dances, gambling, and drugs fall off without a struggle.

The Christian can live a holy life but requires the power of the Holy Spirit. If there is a struggle, a new trip to the altar is needed so all carnality may die. A fresh infilling of the Holy Spirit can liberate a person in a matter of minutes.

Every man can live a life of holiness. There is never any excuse for sin. If a man does not live a holy life, he is inexcusable.

How to Live a Holy Life

There are a few simple rules that will help the Christian live a holy life.

A life of prayer. A prayerless life is always a powerless life. It leads to a cold, carnal profession and worldly conformity.

Prayer is communication and fellowship with Jesus Christ. If one desires to be Christ-like, then he should spend much time communing with Jesus. In sessions of prayer, his heart will glow with love for the Savior.

A fervent desire will be awakened within the Christian as he prays to conform to holiness standards. Not only will the desire for holiness be kindled, but power from on high will be transmitted to the praying child of God enabling him to live victoriously when he arises from his knees.

Bible study. The revelation of God's will begins with His Word. The Christian must be a faithful student of the Bible. Not only should he read the Bible regularly, but he should also attend all Bible studies faithfully. Faithful study of God's Word will add great strength to the child of God.

The Bible teaches clearly the right and wrong regarding most practices. Because of his knowledge of God's Word the Christian will have strong convictions which will keep him true in moments of temptation. Studying God's Word will have a sanctifying influence upon the believer's life. "Sanctify them through thy truth: thy word is truth" (John 17:17). "Now ye are clean through the word which I have spoken unto you" (John 15:3).

God's Word is the source of faith (Romans 10:17). It is impossible to live an overcoming life unless one is strong in faith. In order to please God a person must believe God. There is no better way to develop faith than in the knowledge of the Bible.

Church attendance. A Christian can only become strong as he is faithful in church attendance. Worship and fellowship with others of like faith are essential elements in perfecting holiness in a believer's life. A Christian cannot expect to grow spiritually if he severs his connections with the body. A branch cut from a tree soon dies. Likewise, a Christian separated from the body will soon suffer spiritually. He needs to be faithful in church attendance if he desires to walk with God.

Communicate with the pastor. One of the duties of the pastor is to "perfect" the saints. Lines of communication with the pastor should be maintained for one's own welfare. Confidence in the advice of the man of God is very essential. The believer must learn to talk freely with his pastor concerning his problems and temptations. In sitting in his shepherd's office and listening to the wise counselling of the pastor, the Christian will receive help that can keep him faithful throughout his life.

Be a witness. "And they overcame him by the blood of the Lamb, and by the word of their testimony. . ." (Revelation 12:11). We are endued with power to witness. If that power is not used, the Christian soon becomes anemic. His spiritual muscles become flabby and he has difficulty resisting temptation. God honors our witnessing and gives us a fresh surge of Holy Ghost power. One of the best ways to defeat the devil is to testify of the saving grace of Jesus Christ at every opportunity. The Christian should witness in the home, at work, in church, and on the street.

One day at a time. A young convert may grow discouraged if he thinks that his battle with sinful desires is for a lifetime. He should realize, however, that he lives one day at a time. Each morning he should remind himself that he can live that day for the Lord. If victory is claimed for that day, then it can be claimed for each successive day until one's appetite is set for spiritual things and all desire for worldly pleasure is gone.

Eyes upon Jesus. Jesus is our perfect example. If a person keeps his eyes off the faults of others and his own failures, he will seldom grow discouraged. By keeping his eyes upon Jesus, the child of God is continually inspired to lay aside all worldliness. It will be his delight to maintain high standards of holiness that he might be Christ-like in appearance, conversation, and conduct.

The Bride Makes Herself Ready

"Let us be glad and rejoice, and give honour to him: for the marriage of the Lamb is come, and his wife hath made herself ready" (Revelation 19:7).

The church is the bride of Christ. Paul described the church as being a glorious church without spot or wrinkle (Ephesians 5:27). In Revelation, the bride is described as being arrayed in fine linen, clean and white, which is the righteousness of saints (Revelation 19:8). The bride's wedding garment is evidently righteousness. This righteousness is a purity which will be wholly spotless.

A holy life pays great dividends in this life as well as in eternity. The following are only a few of the blessings the Christian receives in this life:

- He has peace of mind because everything has been made right between himself and God and his fellow man.
- He enjoys better health and generally lives longer. His strength will not be dissipated in sinful pleasures.
- He enjoys a happier home.
- He is more prosperous. He may never become wealthy, but his needs will always be met.
- His life can be more fruitful and rewarding in the service of others. He does not live a selfish, barren life.

As far as eternity is concerned, we may understand the eternal dividends of a holy life by recognizing the promises to the overcomer:

- He will eat of the tree of life (Revelation 2:7).
- He will not be hurt by the second death (Revelation 2:11).
- He will eat of the hidden manna (Revelation 2:17).
- He will be given power over the nations (Revelation 2:26).
- He will be clothed in white raiment (Revelation 3:5).
- He will be made a pillar in the temple of God (Revelation 3:12).
- He will sit with Jesus in His throne (Revelation

3:21).

The greatest reward of all will be to see Jesus and hear Him say, "Well done" (Matthew 25:21). When the saint hears these words from the lips of the Savior, he will know that his life has not been spent in vain. Certainly he will have done well; otherwise the Lord would never tell him that he has done well.

At that moment all the battles and struggles with evil which seem so tremendous now will be as nothing. To enjoy the presence of Jesus will make all of life's troubles worth it all.

Test Your Knowledge

True or False

_____1. God desires for His children to live holy lives of their own volition.

_____2. If a person loves Jesus Christ more than a worldly habit, he will willingly give it up.

_____3. Goals have little importance for a Christian whose life is directed by God.

_____4. Holiness is something that must be perfected, and the responsibility for that perfection within the individual.

_____5. The Scripture "Work out your own salvation. . ." means that every individual decides for himself what program to follow for acquiring salvation.

_____6. The Christian cleanses himself from that which is filthy through repentance.

_____7. The ministry is to help bring the church to perfection.

_____8. Christians can live a holy life without the assistance of the Holy Spirit.

_____9. A prayerless life is always a spiritually powerless life.

_____10. Bible study and church attendance are both vital to any age Christian.

Applying Your Knowledge

This final chapter lists seven areas that should be maintained in order to perfect holiness in our lives. A practical method of monitoring our progress in these areas is to keep a simple diary of some sort. It could be kept in a small book or even in a personal calendar.

List the seven items on each page. They are: (1) Prayer, (2) Bible study, (3) Church attendance, (4) Communication with the pastor, (5) Witnessing, (6) Living one day at a time, and (7) Keeping eyes on Jesus. After you have listed these elements, you can monitor and evaluate your progress on a weekly basis. This will allow you to make necessary adjustments to your life *before* major problems develop.

Prepare yourself for some exciting experiences because walking with Jesus Christ in the path of holiness is exciting!

Expand Your Knowledge

In the areas of holiness, here are some excellent references for further study:

David K. Bernard, *In Search of Holiness*. Word Aflame Press: Hazelwood, 1981.

F. S. Webster, *The Pursuit of Holiness*. Word Aflame Press: Hazelwood, 1982.

Charles F. Stanley, *Handle With Prayer*. Victor Books: Wheaton, 1983.

You may also consider a personal study of the other studies in the Word Aflame Elective Series:

Spiritual Growth and Maturity
Bible Doctrines—The Foundation of the Church
Building Family Relationships
Salvation—The Key to Eternal Life
The Bible—Its Origin and Use
Strategy for Life for Singles and Young Adults
Spiritual Leadership/Successful Soulwinning